THANK YOU FOR YOUR SUPPORT. WE HOPE YOU ENJOY!

DONNELL
&
Courtney

FROM THE FOUNDERS OF
Mr. Baldwin Style

GROOMS

A Professional Stylist's Guide to Wedding Day Apparel for Every Budget

DONNELL BALDWIN & COURTNEY ARRINGTON-BALDWIN

Photography by Alea Lovely

SUTTON PLACE PRESS

SUTTON PLACE PRESS

1040 1st Avenue, Suite #313
New York, NY 10022
WWW.SUTTONPLACEPRESS.COM

Ordering Information:
Quantity sales: Special discounts are available on quantity purchases by corporations, associations, and others. For details, contact the publisher at the address above.
Printed in the United States of America
Library of Congress data available upon request.
First Printing, 2015
ISBN: 978-0-9967275-0-1

Project Manager: Courtney Arrington-Baldwin
Cover Design: Phoebe Flynn Rich
Layout Design and Typesetting: Phoebe Flynn Rich
Image Retouching: Brandon L. Harrison Studio
Editor: Christina Faison
Proofreaders: Chauncey Bellamy, Curtis R. Arrington

To our parents and grandparents,
Thank you for being the outstanding examples of love,
determination, and style that inspired this project.

FOREWORD

A few years ago, I was asked to be a groomsman in a wedding. It was an honor to be included, until I realized what I was expected to wear. As a man who loves style, tailored clothing, and looking distinctive, it was a painful experience for me to wear an outdated rented tux with oversized pants. My wife and I joked that we both could have fit into those trousers. My friends and I looked silly that day, and I thought we resembled poorly dressed clowns, especially next to the beautifully clad women we were escorting down the aisle. I asked my friend how he chose the particular look we sported, and he simply replied, "What else would we have worn?" His answer didn't really surprise me because I hear this response all the time.

I have been a wedding designer for more than ten years, working with couples to create beautiful celebrations that are tailored to their personal style. I often spend months working with a bride to help her locate her perfect gown. Brides try on numerous gown styles, silhouettes, and shades of white, and go from store to store until they find something that truly makes them feel beautiful. So much thought, time, and effort is put into choosing the perfect gown that reflects their individual style. The groom, on the other hand, typically just heads to the local tux shop and quickly settles on a look, probably thinking that all tuxes are the same.

I have often wondered why most men choose something predictable instead of exploring all of the options we have. Shouldn't we put the same amount of thought and care into choosing our wedding attire? I have come to the conclusion that most grooms simply don't know their options—that they are also allowed to showcase individual style.

Men have options, and *GROOMS* shows us what those options are. The following pages will help you think beyond a rented tux by giving you permission to be fashionable and think outside of the box. This book will help you define your personal style while teaching you how to customize it to the style of your wedding. From classic to preppy and island to rustic, you will be able to master the details of your wedding day attire and set yourself apart as a stylish groom.

—*Steve Moore,* Owner of *Sinclair & Moore*

TO THE BRIDE & GROOM

Congratulations! The hardest part is complete: you have identified one another as soul mates. The magical proposal went off without a hitch, hopefully (if not, at least she said "Yes"). Now it is time to navigate the nuptials. The wedding date is set. The bride's gown is ordered. But wait! What about the groom? What is the man of the hour planning to wear? By now, both of you have probably discussed the groom's attire, or maybe it is still on the ever-growing "To Do" list. With all the planning and preparation, perhaps you can use some help. We created this book to provide grooms with the necessary styling tips and tools to use in preparation for "the big day." Not only is this a guidebook for planning your wedding day attire, it can also be used for style inspiration. Within these pages are various looks that will provide grooms with visual guidance and advice for selecting the perfect look.

Generally speaking, ladies are very specific about their wedding gowns. For many brides, they have been dreaming about this day since they were young girls. A bride can, typically, find a close replica of her dream gown and can choose from various options and styles—whether from a custom design, a major retailer, or a bridal gown boutique. However, grooms are normally pointed in one direction–the tuxedo rental shop. Many are never made aware that they, too, have options.

Before you head toward the traditional route of "tux-renting," have you ever stopped to consider if a tuxedo is really what you want for your wedding? How about how you will distinguish yourself from the groomsmen? Well, do not fret. This book addresses many topics to keep in mind before you settle on a wedding day look. You will also find tips on how to look amazing on any budget. Plus, we have secrets on selecting quality pieces that can be reused long after the wedding is done. By the time you finish this book, you will be equipped to decide what to wear, where to find it, and how to wear it.

LETTER TO GROOMS

Greetings to my fellow gentlemen of style! Listen, your wedding is a very important day that you will remember forever. As a husband, you will be taking on a new level of responsibility and commitment, making vows that are serious and binding. Not to scare you, but this is a big deal! Do not worry, though; marriage is a beautiful and great decision. Trust me.

I cannot stress enough the importance of looking your best for your wedding day. Guests, from various stages and phases of your lives, are gathering to witness your union, which means the spotlight is on both of you. This may be the only time that you and your bride will have all of these people in the same space, ever, so let's make sure you are dressed for the occasion.

While this day is usually about the bride, remember, it is your day, too. You should not look like you just showed up. Believe me, once you discover how much energy and resources your future bride spends on her hair, make-up, nails, gown, and alterations, you are going to be glad that you took the time and effort to not look like you threw something together (or rented a tuxedo from a dodgy rental shop, for goodness sake).

I have worked in menswear for some time—most recently as a Styling Manager for Ralph Lauren and a Styling Editor for a global e-commerce retailer. Outside of my work with fashion models, I have seen, and worked with, many gentlemen who struggle to pull their wedding day looks together. With so much to think about, you can't allow your attire to add to the stress. For the remainder of this book, the Mr. Baldwin Style team will guide you through the journey of selecting your wedding day look. We will be your personal wardrobe stylists providing you with options for just about every type of wedding, even if on a strict budget. If you are still stumped after reading this book, you can always contact us. We will be more than happy to assist you in pulling together those loose ends. Don't fret, grooms—you're in good hands!

Now, let's get you inspired and dressed for the big day!

—*Donnell*

GETTING STARTED

Grooms, consider the following topics as you plan and purchase items for your wedding day attire:

- Style or Theme
- Venue and Level of Formality
- Bride's Look
- Number of Looks
- Budget
- Body Type and Appearance
- Attendants' Apparel
- Schedule

Style or Theme

Have you and your bride identified a wedding style or theme for your big day? This can be as simple as "we want a garden wedding" or as specific as "we want a Great Gatsby-themed wedding." Remember, this is different from identifying wedding colors. The theme will often dictate the wedding location, along with almost every other detail surrounding the wedding—from the flowers to the dinner menu.

Venue and Level of Formality

Has your wedding venue been selected? Will the ceremony take place in one location and the reception in another? The venue will likely determine the level of formality of your wedding and the day's attire. If the ceremony and reception locations differ in formality, you may need to change your look, or add or subtract pieces, to make sure you are appropriate for both locations. For example, if your ceremony is held in a cathedral and the reception in a rustic barn, it is likely that you will need, or want to, modify your look to fit both locations. Typically, the level of formality will fall within one of five categories: casual, semi-formal, formal, black tie, and, in rare occasions, white tie. (Refer to the "Styling Tips" chapter for more details on levels of formality.)

Bride's Look

Traditionally, the bride's wedding day look is a surprise to the groom and is not revealed until the bride walks down the aisle. Grooms, there is no reason to part from that tradition just to pick out your wedding day attire. However, you can ask your bride key questions that will not give away the surprise, such as: Will your gown be full length? Will it be white, ivory, or another color? Are you planning to have a reception look? When we style grooms for their wedding day, the bride will share photos of her gown with us, so we can ensure that the groom's look is in sync with hers.

Number of Looks

As a general rule, the number of looks that the groom has for the wedding day festivities should be less than or equal to the number of the bride's looks. If the bride has one look for the day, then the groom should only have one. Although the day is about the both of you, the bride should be the focus, and the groom should be her perfect complement in style, elegance, and formality. Avoid those wild or trendy looks. The only people you are allowed to outshine are your groomsmen and guests.

Budget

It is commonly known that weddings can be very expensive. Often the groom's attire falls low in priority for the wedding day budget. Typically, for her wedding day attire, the bride spends seven to ten times the amount of the groom. Ouch! However, we are here to show you that it is entirely possible to look appropriate and debonair for your wedding day without breaking the bank. That is why it is important, early on, to identify your attire budget, be it big or small.

Body Type and Appearance

When selecting your wedding day attire, you should consider your body type, skin tone, and overall style. Hopefully, now being an adult, you have grown comfortable with the body that you were given (or at least the things that you can't change). You have to accept that some things are suited for you, and some things are not. In other words, work with what you have. Pick items that complement your finest qualities and will allow you to feel your best on your special day.

Attendants' Apparel

Early on in the attire planning process, you should think about whether or not you would like your groomsmen and best man to be dressed similarly to you or in something completely different. Either way, you will need to have something that distinguishes you as the groom, even if it is a small change. It is best to communicate your wishes to your attendants as early as possible. For example, if you decide to have everyone wear the same suit as you, your attendants must agree to your same general budget.

Schedule

This one is pretty simple: keep a schedule when planning your wedding day attire. If a custom suit or tuxedo is what you want for your wedding, you must plan for the lead-time associated with custom suiting, which can range from six to twelve weeks, in most instances. However, if you had a short engagement period or started planning your attire late, then a custom suit might not be the best choice for you.

After careful consideration of each topic above, you will begin to narrow down your wedding attire options until you finally land on a selection that is perfect for you on your special day.

THE
CLASSIC
GROOM

GET THE LOOK

Black Notch Lapel Tuxedo Jacket

Black Flat Front Tuxedo Pants

White Tuxedo Shirt

Black Silk Self-Tie Bow Tie

Black Silk Knot Stud Set

Black Silk Knot Cufflinks

Black Dress Socks

Black Round Toe Calf
Lace-Up Shoe

Black and White Silk Polka Dot
Pocket Square

Black Braces with Contrasting
White Ears

Floral Boutonnière

THE CLASSIC GROOM

A groom who chooses the more classic or traditional route for his wedding day attire is a dashing gentleman. When we think of the Classic Groom, we imagine a sleek, sophisticated man with no fuss or frills—only the refined basics. The Classic Groom is appropriately dressed for the occasion without too much deviation. He is not trying to follow the latest trend.

If it's a black tie wedding, expect to see him in black tie attire. This groom understands the formal nature of his wedding and expects that his bride has plans to wear a formal gown. The Classic Groom usually refrains from the fuss of what to wear, yet he knows that he wants to look sharp on his wedding day. He might add a bit of flare with his accessory choices, but overall, he tends to be more conservative.

LOOK ONE

One option for the Classic Groom is the standard black tuxedo, which has been a staple in fashion since the 1800s. The groom pictured here is styled in a black tuxedo with a crisp white tux shirt and black silk self-tie bow tie—a very clean look. We embellished the tuxedo shirt with black silk knot studs in place of standard white buttons. Note that silk knot studs pull together the look by adding a bit of visual detail to the shirt and at the wrists, in lieu of standard cufflinks. If a classic look has worked for the likes of presidents, dignitaries, and royalty for hundreds of years, it will certainly work for your wedding.

Balancing a classic look is not very challenging. In fact, any traditional gentleman could achieve this look; the key to remember is fit. Fit has the ability to make or break an entire outfit. Often,

tuxedo rental companies do not have many options for alterations other than the sleeve and pant length. Our ultimate recommendation is that you buy your own tuxedo. If you choose to purchase from a local retailer, make sure you consult with a good tailor who can alter the tuxedo to make it look custom-made for you. On the other hand, if you want to spend a bit more for a made-to-measure or bespoke tuxedo, make sure you are comfortable with the suit maker you've selected. Be sure to review your desired fit with him or her and provide reference images showing how you want the tuxedo to fit.

The best thing about selecting a tuxedo for your wedding day is its versatility. It is an investment that will last you for years to come—from one formal event to another. Remember, for the Classic Groom, less is more.

Master the Details

Tuxedo Pants

For a more contemporary look, select a flat front pant without pleats. Trust us, it will keep you from looking like a grandpa.

Tuxedo Shirt

Select an appropriate fitting tuxedo shirt. The shirt should fit your neck, sleeve length, and torso properly. When the top button is fastened, you should be able to get no more than your index and middle fingers between your neck and shirt collar. With your arms down at your side, the sleeve of the shirt should fall to the wrist crease on the inside of your arm where your wrist and hand meet. With your arms still down, the sleeves on the tuxedo jacket should fall above the shirt with no more than one inch of the shirt showing beyond the jacket. If you have difficulty finding a shirt that meets all of these suggestions, consider purchasing a shirt that can be taken to a local tailor for adjustments. For a larger budget, simply purchase a custom-made tuxedo shirt.

Braces

For a gentleman with a taller, slimmer physique, consider a cummerbund as an alternative to braces (suspenders). Choose either braces or a cummerbund, but never both.

Boutonnière

The boutonnière should always be placed on the left lapel of a gentleman's jacket to cover the buttonhole stitch.

Groomsmen

Consider styling the groomsmen in the same tuxedo style as the groom. If the groomsmen opt for a less expensive tuxedo, make sure the color, style of the jacket lapel, and fit of the tuxedo pants are the same as the groom's. To distinguish the groom from his attendants, consider having them wear plain white dress shirts without the pleats and stud set. They can also have different floral boutonnières, either a different flower or the same flower in a different color.

WHERE TO WEAR

The traditional black tuxedo can be worn for just about any wedding, as long as you match the formality of your bride. We recommend these venue types:

- Formal indoor wedding: hotel grand ballroom, country club, university club, grand library, museum, concert hall, or restaurant

- Formal outdoor wedding: castle, estate, city rooftop, or botanical garden

WAYS TO SAVE

- If the budget for your wedding day attire is not quite suited for a custom tuxedo, purchase an off-the-rack tuxedo at a local retailer and have it tailored. If you are a smaller guy, choose a slim fit.

- Purchase silk knot cufflinks instead of the traditional metal ones. Silk knot cufflinks are classy and cost at least half the price of most traditional cufflinks.

- Purchase a simple round toe, leather lace-up shoe, in lieu of a patent leather tuxedo shoe. Well after the wedding, they can be worn for business or other formal occasions.

GET THE LOOK

White Tuxedo Shirt with
French Cuffs

Black and White Glen Plaid,
Diamond Tip Bow Tie

Black Velvet Waistcoat

Black Slim Fit Tuxedo Pants with
Single Satin Side Stripe

Vintage Gold and Black Onyx
Cufflinks

Gold Pocket Watch or
Gold Link Watch

Black Leather or Patent Leather
Rounded Toe Shoe

LOOK TWO

If you want a slightly different touch to your look, add a waistcoat. Also known as vests, waistcoats are one of our style essentials; in fact, we suggest them for stepping up the classic tuxedo a notch. Waistcoats have been a part of men's fashion since the 1600s. When styled correctly, they can be very appropriate for the Classic Groom.

If you and your groomsmen decide to go with a waistcoat, resist the temptation to match it to the wedding colors or decor. Certainly do not attempt to match the bridesmaids' dresses, either. It will end up looking like a late '80s or '90s prom, and that is not the look we are going for, here. If a waistcoat is not included in your tuxedo purchase, make sure you select one that is close to the color of your tux. For the Classic Groom, the waistcoat is ideally black.

In this section, we have selected a classic black velvet waistcoat with a black satin lapel. We also included a classic white tuxedo shirt, black tuxedo pants, and black leather rounded toe shoes. Notice that there is something regal about this look. To complement the Victorian look while maintaining the contemporary flair of the waistcoat, we selected gold accoutrements (a pocket watch and cufflinks) for an added element of refinement.

The gold pocket watch shown is a vintage find. Typically, pocket watches are worn exactly as they are described—in the pocket. While styling rules are open to creative interpretation, please keep in mind that pocket watches take the place of wearing a wristwatch, so choose one or the other. If the pocket watch is a little too vintage for your style, choose a gold link wristwatch, as shown in the image. (Please see photos with both options.)

Also, to add to the gold accoutrements, we selected vintage gold and black onyx cufflinks, which can be a great addition to your look, especially if they are meaningful and special. Some grooms will use the cufflinks from their fathers or grandfathers for sentimental reasons, whereas other grooms will purchase vintage cufflinks simply because they are unique and not mass produced. Either way, make sure your cufflinks are not an eyesore but complement the bride and the formality of the occasion.

Instead of the standard black necktie or black bow tie, we selected a glen plaid, diamond tip bow tie. This choice adds a bit of variation to the traditional black tie attire but is still very appropriate for the occasion. Glen plaid, polka dot, pin dot, or any type of black and white pattern will work handsomely with this look.

For the Classic Groom, the waistcoat provides a polished look and can be worn on its own or with a tuxedo jacket. If you and your bride decide to have a second look on your wedding day, the waistcoat with tuxedo pants is a great alternative for your reception. Be sure to make your entrance into the reception wearing the tuxedo jacket, and then remove it when appropriate.

Master the Details

Tuxedo Shirt

In lieu of switching out the standard shirt buttons with a stud set, consider keeping the standard buttons, which will not compete with the ones on the vest.

Fabric

Make sure the waistcoat material is appropriate for the season of your wedding. The waistcoat shown in this section is velvet with a satin trim, making it most appropriate for a fall, winter, or cooler climate wedding.

Fit

Select a waistcoat that is long enough to cover the waistline of your pants and will not show any of the tuxedo shirt. Also, make sure to adjust the belt in the back of the waistcoat to achieve the proper fit. You'll want the waistcoat to be fitted to your torso but not so tight that it pulls the buttons.

Buttons

For a five-button waistcoat, the last button should be left unfastened in accordance with tradition and standard etiquette. As an option, the top button can be left undone, as well.

Boutonnière

Adding a floral boutonnière to a waistcoat can be very tricky, especially if the flowers in the boutonnière are too large. As an alternative to the floral boutonnière, consider a small lapel pin or simply nothing at all. The pocket watch and/or cufflinks may be enough for the look.

Groomsmen

If you opt for a waistcoat, consider styling your groomsmen in the same vest but without the pocket watch and patterned bow tie. The groomsmen can be styled in simple black satin self-tie bow ties.

WHERE TO WEAR

The black waistcoat option with a black tuxedo can be worn for a classic style wedding. We recommend it as a second look, for the reception, or a groomsmen look for one of the following venue types:

- Formal indoor wedding or reception: estate ballroom, hotel ballroom, country club, university club, grand library, museum, concert hall, or restaurant

- Formal outdoor wedding or reception: castle, estate, city rooftop, or botanical garden

WAYS TO SAVE

- Do a little vintage shopping at a local thrift store or flea market for a nice pair of vintage cufflinks or a vintage pocket watch.

- Skip purchasing a stud set, and keep the buttons that came with the tuxedo shirt.

GET THE LOOK

White Dinner Jacket with
Shawl Collar

Black Slim Fit Tuxedo Pants with
Single Satin Side Stripe

White Tuxedo Shirt with
French Cuffs

Black Onyx Stud Set and Cufflinks

Black Satin Self-Tie Bow Tie

Silk Black and White Polka Dot
Pocket Square

Oxblood Velvet Bloom Lapel Pin

LOOK THREE

The white dinner jacket has a history that dates back to the early 1900s. You may be familiar with the white dinner jacket worn by Humphrey Bogart in *Casablanca* or the one worn by Sean Connery as James Bond. In its origin, the white dinner jacket was usually worn for social gatherings during the summer months or in warmer climates. However, today, many gentlemen have disregarded the seasons and just wear the jacket year round.

For this Classic Groom look, we styled the groom with a white dinner jacket instead of a black tuxedo jacket. We selected a shawl collar dinner jacket, which gives an air of sophistication. This collar type is reminiscent of smoking jackets from the Victorian era, giving the appearance of the highest level of formality without wearing a tuxedo jacket with tails. To elevate the distinction of this look, we used an oxblood velvet bloom lapel pin in lieu of a floral boutonnière. We also added a silk polka dot pocket square. Instead of a standard necktie, we used a bow tie, which is appropriate to wear at this level of formality. When opting for a dinner jacket, the possibility of wearing anything other than a bow tie should be rethought. Wearing a necktie may suggest that you are unaware of proper etiquette.

The black tuxedo pants and black patent leather derby shoes anchor the look while complementing the black bow tie. As an alternative, you could select an off-white dinner jacket and style it with navy or midnight blue tuxedo pants. In that instance, we recommend wearing a navy bow tie for consistency.

Before settling on a white dinner jacket for your wedding day, make sure that this look will complement your bride's gown. Although your bride may not disclose full details, confirm that her gown is formal, and that the white dinner jacket is appropriate for your wedding. If your bride is planning to wear a tea-length dress, which is indicative of a semi-formal wedding, a different jacket should be considered.

When shopping for a white dinner jacket, pay careful attention to the fabric. A fabric that is too thin may show the inner lining of the garment when worn, which is not ideal. It may end up looking poorly constructed. Therefore, look for dinner jackets in lightweight wool or linen/cotton blends for the warmer months. The white dinner jacket is a great option for the Classic Groom who wants to vary a bit from the traditional black tuxedo without going overboard.

Master the Details

Contrasting Lapel
Contrasting lapels on tuxedo jackets are a great way to add a bit of detail to your overall look. You can achieve this with a black satin lapel; however, you could go with a navy lapel. Either way, consider keeping the lapel dark to match the pants and bow tie of your tuxedo. Otherwise, you could run the risk of looking too trendy.

Dress Shirts
Avoid patterned or dark colored dress shirts when wearing a white dinner jacket. Darker colors and patterns take away from the classic look and may even show through the white jacket.

Waistcoats
A waistcoat is not a necessity. The white dinner jacket already makes a strong statement. If you decide to add a waistcoat, consider adding one with a half-moon shaped neckline that does not interfere with the look of the dinner jacket and the shawl collar.

Belt
Skip the belt. If you are wearing classic tuxedo pants, they should be tailored to you without the requirement of a belt. Keep it simple by not adding extra items that will "date" your look in the future.

Shoes
As an alternative to lace-up shoes, black patent leather or black velvet loafers are a nice complement to a white or off-white dinner jacket. Loafers are very classy and keep with the sophisticated look of the dinner jacket.

Groomsmen
The white dinner jacket should be reserved for the groom only. In styling the wedding party, the groom should stand out from the remainder of the gentlemen. Our preference would be to style the groom with a white dinner jacket and the groomsmen in black tuxedo jackets—both with the same lapel profile.

WHERE TO WEAR

The white dinner jacket should be worn at the most formal of weddings and can be used as a reception option if you plan to wear the classic black tuxedo for the ceremony. We recommend the following venue types:

- Formal indoor wedding: country club, university club, grand library, museum, concert hall, or estate

- Formal outdoor wedding: manor, estate, city rooftop, botanical garden, or yacht

WAYS TO SAVE

- Purchase a full black tuxedo. It is typically less expensive to purchase a full tuxedo, rather than the pieces separately. Purchase the white dinner jacket as a separate item. Even if you do not plan to wear the black tuxedo jacket for your wedding, you will have the full tuxedo for future formal events. It is unlikely that you will wear the white dinner jacket as often as a full black tuxedo.

THE
CLASSIC
GROOM
REMIXED

GET THE LOOK

Black Velvet Peak Lapel
Tuxedo Jacket

Black Cotton Blend Turtleneck

Black Tuxedo Pants

Black Leather Lace-Up Shoes

Silk Black and White Herringbone
Pocket Square

Silver Link Wristwatch

Floral Boutonnière

THE CLASSIC GROOM REMIXED

You might be wondering what exactly is the Classic Groom Remixed? Well, it is exactly as it sounds. This groom is the classic guy who incorporates non-traditional elements to his look. Tradition gets an upgrade. He wants to remain classic and timeless yet also appreciates a bit of flare to his wedding look. The Classic Groom Remixed has a conservative sensibility but enjoys mixing it up to avoid predictability. Besides, where is the fun in being predictable? These looks are perfect for the guy who is preparing either to elope abroad or to have a full ceremony with family and friends gathered to share the moment.

For a fall or winter wedding, a tuxedo jacket in black velvet is a good option. A black velvet tuxedo jacket with a satin lapel is a game-changing piece that can be difficult to successfully pull off. Velvet tuxedo jackets are classic formal wear with added texture and warmth for the colder months.

This particular look pairs the classic black tuxedo with a black turtleneck, giving a chic and fashion-forward look. The turtleneck is a clear departure from the classic combination of a white tuxedo shirt, black bow tie, and studs. For finishing touches, we added a black and white silk herringbone pocket square. It's simple and very elegant. Your bride and guests will love your sleek, sophisticated look.

WHERE TO WEAR

This black on black tux look is for a very classy yet fashionable wedding. We recommend the following venue types:

- Indoor wedding: church, university club, historic inn, historic hotel, or historic library

WAYS TO SAVE

- If you choose a custom velvet jacket or an off-the-rack velvet jacket on the pricier side, consider purchasing a less expensive, good quality pair of tuxedo pants from a discount menswear store or retailer. With the velvet jacket, it is easier to mix and match pieces than with a standard black tuxedo.

- A nice cotton blend turtleneck is ordinarily less expensive than a standard tuxedo shirt.

Master the Details

Dress Shoes

We have styled this look with black leather lace-up shoes. However, another option is a black patent leather or black velvet loafer. If you elect to wear velvet loafers, choose the color carefully. With an all-black look, black velvet loafers are most appropriate. Do not introduce another color.

Accessories

Keep the accessories to a minimum. The all-black look already has a very sleek and classy sensibility. There is no need for flash and glitz. Let the texture and refinement of the velvet speak for itself. You can add a patterned pocket square, as we did with the herringbone print, to break up the monochromatic look. Other than that, keep it simple.

Boutonnière

Refrain from having a large bouquet of flowers on your lapel. A misconception is that the artistry of your bridal florist has to be shown. We like the look of a simple ivory rose bud, giving a nice contrast to the black. It also maintains a classic appearance. One single rose or carnation will do the trick. We recommend trying a smaller one— a little bit goes a long way.

Groomsmen

With this remixed look, your groomsmen should wear a classic black tuxedo with the same lapel profile as your velvet jacket. Rather than matching your black turtleneck, the groomsmen should wear solid black dress shirts with the first two buttons undone. Since you chose to wear a turtleneck in place of a bow tie, it is very appropriate for the attendants to be styled without ties, as well. They will still match your level of formality, but you will stand out as the groom.

GET THE LOOK

Black Notch Lapel Tuxedo Jacket

Black Flat Front Tuxedo Pants

Pink Dress Shirt with
Contrasting Collar

Black Silk Self-Tie Bow Tie

Black Velvet Loafers

White Cotton Pocket Square

Floral Boutonnière

LOOK TWO

The classic tuxedo has been around seemingly forever. We have all seen changes in trends, including fit, lapel size, fuller cuts, slim cuts, and the list goes on as fashion evolves. The standard black tuxedo look with a classic white shirt can be a bit expected. Have you ever thought about wearing a pastel colored shirt with your tuxedo? Here, we chose a pink oxford shirt with a white contrast collar to remix the traditional vibe. This subtle hint of color really comes off effortlessly. We paired this shirt with a black bow tie and white pocket square. We added velvet loafers with no socks. Remember the key to a classic remixed look is to incorporate small, impactful changes to your already traditional tuxedo look.

Master the Details

Colored Dress Shirt

Branching out and trying new things can be exciting. For the combination of a black tuxedo and colored shirt, we recommend pastel colors for the shirt with contrasting collars in white. See which color looks best on you and works best for the other color accents in your wedding. We used pink, but maybe you would look great in a canary yellow or light blue.

Pocket Square

A simple white pocket square to match the white collar of the shirt gives a nice clean look. The square fold helps to maintain the formality.

Socks

We prefer this look without dress socks. If you are going to add dress socks, consider wearing black socks to match the pants and shoes.

Velvet Loafers

Velvet loafers are a very sophisticated choice of footwear that reached popularity in the early 1900s. They are elegant and often adorned with gold bullion embellishments across the bridge of the shoe. If you are not particularly keen on the ornate, you can find these without all of the accents. Either way, velvet loafers are a great option to elevate your look.

Groomsmen

You will stand out quite well in your colored shirt, just as a groom should. Leave the groomsmen classically styled in white tuxedo shirts with white club collars and your same bow tie. This way there is uniformity, but the subtle difference will be your pop of color.

WHERE TO WEAR

This Classic Remixed look with a contrast collar shirt is appropriate in many settings where the Classic Groom looks are also appropriate. We recommend the following venue types:

- Formal indoor wedding: hotel grand ballroom, country club, university club, grand library, museum, or restaurant

- Formal outdoor wedding: estate or city rooftop

WAYS TO SAVE

- If you plan to wear velvet loafers, which can be quite expensive, purchase your loafers during early spring when end of season sales of winter merchandise occur. However, you may need to plan your apparel well in advance of your wedding day.

- Purchasing a contrasting collar shirt will be a great addition to your wardrobe and can be worn year-round with other clothing that is less formal than a tuxedo.

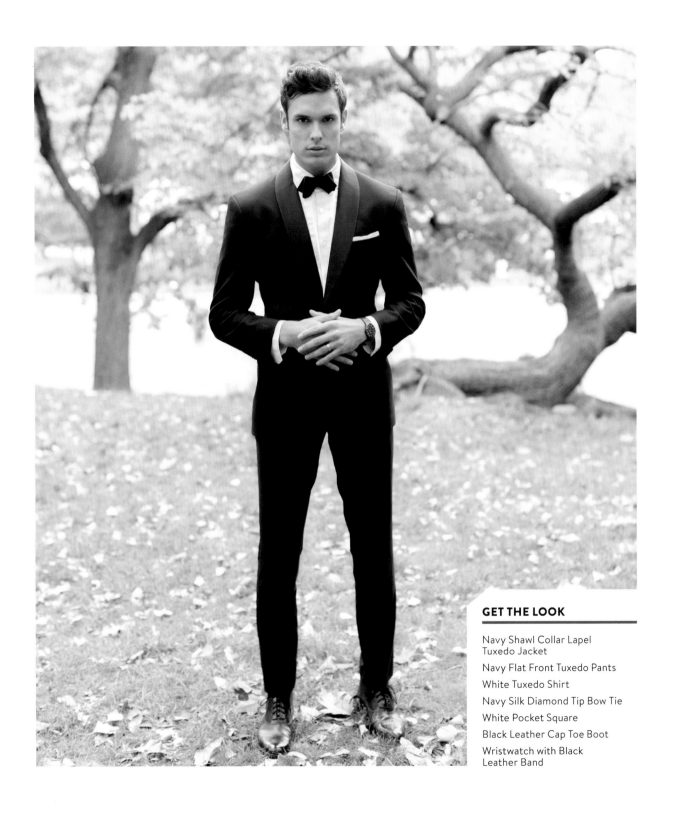

GET THE LOOK

Navy Shawl Collar Lapel
Tuxedo Jacket

Navy Flat Front Tuxedo Pants

White Tuxedo Shirt

Navy Silk Diamond Tip Bow Tie

White Pocket Square

Black Leather Cap Toe Boot

Wristwatch with Black
Leather Band

ONE TUXEDO THREE WAYS

Many classic grooms gravitate toward the standard black tuxedo. A Classic Groom Remixed really enjoys the safety of the classic style, but is willing to explore other options. This tuxedo is navy— a very popular color for wedding tuxes recently. Here, we show three great ways to wear a navy tuxedo:

Navy Tuxedo and White Tuxedo Shirt

One classic way to style this tuxedo is with a traditional formal white tuxedo shirt and navy bow tie. The beauty of wearing this tux in a traditional way is that it exudes elegance and class, in addition to working just as well as a black tuxedo. We chose a classic white pocket square to keep the look simple. There is dignity in simplicity in this timeless look.

Navy Tuxedo and Black Shirt

Another great way to wear this tuxedo is by adding a simple black dress shirt into the mix; this changes the look entirely. Whether you decide to wear a silk black bow tie or necktie, this simple style variation makes this look more sleek and chic. We added a black silk pocket square for color consistency and a slight touch of detail. With more of a European sensibility, this look will confirm you as a modern groom. It could be a reception or after-party look if you want to change throughout the wedding day.

Navy Tuxedo and Chambray Shirt

Lose the formality; lose the tie; and bring on the denim! We show the same tuxedo look with a chambray shirt. Denim has a great way of being stylishly evergreen, timeless, and limitless. A chambray shirt will work with virtually any pairing of your choice. If this look will work for your wedding, we encourage you to try it. It is a definite head turner and an attention grabber.

Master the Details

Tuxedo Shirt

If adding a black or chambray shirt under the navy tuxedo is just too much for you, consider getting a white tuxedo shirt made from a textured material. Pique fabric adds nice detailing without changing the color of your dress shirt. It will not be noticeable from far off, but as your guests come closer to greet you, your eye for details will pleasantly surprise them.

Lapel

A nice option to create a full monochromatic look is to select a navy tuxedo with a navy satin lapel instead of the black lapel, shown in this look. Since these tuxedos are a little more difficult to find, it may be worth it to go the custom route.

Tuxedo Pants

The tuxedo pants selected here were designed without the satin or grosgrain trim on the side, which is traditional for tuxedo pants. This is one of the elements that allows this navy tuxedo to work with a black dress shirt, as well as a chambray shirt. If there were black trim on the side of the pants, the colored shirts may compete with the tuxedo pant detailing.

Pocket Square

If you choose a dress shirt in a non-traditional color, consider changing the pocket square from classic white, used to complement the white tuxedo shirt, to another color or pattern. We selected black to match the lapel of the tuxedo jacket with the black shirt and chambray shirt looks.

Groomsmen

We recommend styling the groomsmen in your same navy tuxedo. To distinguish you as the groom, you could have them wear silk or knit neckties instead of a bowtie. If you prefer the attendants in bow ties, consider selecting bow ties or pocket squares with a small pin dot pattern for a subtle difference.

WHERE TO WEAR

The navy tuxedo is a great option for the Classic Groom Remixed and is appropriate for many wedding styles and locations. We recommend the following venue types:

- Formal indoor wedding: church, hotel grand ballroom, country club, grand library, museum, or estate

- Formal outdoor wedding: estate, city rooftop, or winery

WAYS TO SAVE

- Changing your shirt from a white tuxedo to a black dress or chambray shirt provides inexpensive options for a second (and even a third) look for your wedding day.

- When looking for a navy bow tie, search online retailers that have good quality self-tie bow ties. Sometimes the best deals are not found from the well-known menswear retailers.

GET THE LOOK (option)

Instead of a standard white tuxedo shirt and white pocket square, consider a black dress shirt and black pocket square.

GET THE LOOK (option)

In lieu of the standard white tuxedo shirt and white pocket square, consider a chambray shirt and black pocket square.

THE
CHIC
GROOM

GET THE LOOK

Gray Peak Lapel Slim Fit Suit
White Pleated Front Tuxedo Shirt
Gray Knit Necktie
Gray Burlap Bloom Lapel Pin
Black Silk Knot Cuff Links
Black Leather Lace-Up Shoe

THE CHIC GROOM

If the thought of satin lapels and patent leather shoes gives you hives, you may be a Chic Groom. You want the polished look of a suit but do not desire the commitment of a tuxedo. Your wedding venue and style are likely between semi-formal and formal, which for you, definitely does not dictate black-tie dress. A suit that will be a workhorse in your wardrobe after the wedding is your idea of a perfect purchase.

It's no secret that we are big fans of the color gray. It is neutral, fresh, and timeless, when styled appropriately. Gray suits (and tuxedos) are great for numerous occasions, especially your nuptials. Since gray pairs beautifully with bridal gowns in white or ivory, it gives the couple a soft, romantic option rather than dressing in the same color. If you feel that black is too harsh for the style of your wedding, and khaki is just too preppy, consider the luminous color of gray. As with most of our suit and tuxedo recommendations, we prefer that you purchase, instead of renting, your gray suit and have it altered by a tailor you trust to complement your physique.

There are a few things that help distinguish this look for your wedding day, so that it does not look like something for just another day at the office. One way is to choose a peak lapel suit with a single button. This combination is often considered more formal than a notched lapel with two buttons; both details are found more commonly in tuxedos. Also, the addition of a tuxedo shirt with pleats and French cuffs in place of the standard dress shirt helps to enhance the look. Selecting a gray knit necktie to match with the gray suit helps to further deviate this look from a business one. Monochromatic looks often feel chic because they are easy on the eyes, without a lot of patterns and prints competing for attention.

We offered another alternative to the necktie by replacing it with a gray silk bow tie. This option keeps the monochromatic color theme but elevates the element of formality, especially with the black tuxedo shirt buttons. A tuxedo shirt with a pleated front and black buttons is one of our new favorite styles for semi-formal weddings. The black buttons provide the similar look of a stud set without the fuss of exchanging them. To match the shirt buttons and add a bit of whimsy, we added a print pocket square complementing the wedding colors and theme. As can be seen from the images, a gray peak lapel suit can provide versatility for a semi-formal wedding and work well for an outdoor event.

WHERE TO WEAR

The gray peak lapel suit is an appropriate option for the Chic Groom. We recommend the following venues:

- Chic indoor wedding: church, private residence, hotel, grand tent, or museum

- Chic outdoor wedding: vineyard, botanical garden, or sculpture garden

WAYS TO SAVE

- Purchase a tuxedo shirt with black buttons. By purchasing this more contemporary shirt, you will save the cost of purchasing a stud set.

- Purchasing a knit necktie in place of a standard silk or wool necktie should result in cost savings. Knit ties are often less expensive than the standard silk and wool alternatives.

Master the Details

Peak Lapels

As previously mentioned, peak lapels are a more formal option than notch lapels. When selecting a peak lapel suit, consider the width of the lapel. Wider lapels have been a recent trend but tend to be more appropriate for those with an average to larger physique. If you are a guy with a smaller chest, you may want to consider selecting a narrower lapel, so that it does not appear that you have on your dad's jacket.

Fabric

When selecting a gray suit, make sure to consider fabric options. If your wedding is in the spring or summer, lightweight cotton or linen blend fabrics will be fine. For weddings in cooler climates, consider wool blend materials. In addition to a heavier fabric, you may want to choose darker shades of gray for winter weddings.

Tie Dimple

When wearing a necktie, even a knit one, make sure to put a dimple in the tie just below the knot. This is the sign of a true gentleman and adds detail to the necktie.

Shoes

When pairing shoes with gray suits, there a few color options. Because we were attempting to replicate a tuxedo look, we went with a black shoe. In general we prefer the darker, richer tones of brown, cordovan, and black to ensure that the look is wedding appropriate and does not appear as if you are going to the office.

Groomsmen

Style your groomsmen in the same gray peak lapel suit. To distinguish you as the groom, request that they wear black knit neckties, which will be a small deviation from your gray knit necktie. With the bow tie option, the groomsmen can wear gray neckties if you are wearing the gray silk bow tie.

GET THE LOOK (option)

In lieu of the gray knit necktie and the gray burlap bloom lapel pin shown previously, a gray silk bow tie and silk print pocket square can be used to complete this look. The bow tie is more formal, and may be better for a groom who prefers to wear a bow tie on his wedding day. In this option, we have also eliminated the boutonnière for a cleaner look.

GET THE LOOK

Black Notch Lapel Slim Fit Suit
White Pleated Front Tuxedo Shirt
Black Silk-Blend Necktie
Black Silk Pocket Square
Black Leather Lace-Up Shoe
White Bronze Lion Pin
White Bronze Lion Cufflinks

LOOK TWO

The black suit is probably the most versatile of all chic looks that you could choose for your wedding day. A black suit can work for just about any occasion and looks quite appropriate. To dress up the look, we have added a necktie also in black. Choosing a necktie (or bow tie) that is the same color as the suit will allow the look to be more formal, especially if you do not want to wear a tuxedo. We recommend sticking with either a white shirt or a black-and-white Bengal striped shirt. Any other color may look too much like office attire. Here, the groom is shown with a tuxedo shirt that helps to elevate the look, making it more wedding appropriate. Traditionally, bow ties are worn with tuxedo shirts, but we decided to break the rules a bit by adding a necktie with this pleated shirt. We really like how the necktie complements the vertical pleats. Do not be afraid to break the rules every now and then. Remember to give it a try before your actual wedding day to make sure you like the look.

What a great look for an elopement! Less is more. You don't have to wear a tuxedo, but with these options, you will have a semi-formal look that is appropriate for City Hall or a smaller wedding at a historic home. This look will achieve maximum style with minimal effort. You will thank us later.

Master the Details

Tie Pin

In lieu of using a tie bar or collar pin to accessorize the necktie, we used a white bronze lion pin. Pins are nice accessories for the Chic Groom, as they can be used on a necktie or on the lapel of a jacket instead of a boutonnière. As an alternative to a lion, you could use a pin with greater personal significance, like a family crest.

Pocket Square

To keep the look clean and monochromatic, opt for a black pocket square with a puff fold. This is a bit more casual than the formal square fold and more visible with the black pocket square against the black suit jacket due to the texture of the puff. In addition to providing a delightful look, the puff fold is one of the more easy folds to achieve.

Shoes

Avoid the temptation to wear a shoe in a color other than black. For this wedding day look, keep it clean with a nice black leather blucher or oxford shoe.

Boutonnière

For this look, we opted to forego a floral boutonnière. If you or the bride feel that a boutonnière is necessary, remember to go small. A flower like a bud from a tea rose will suffice. Because we have added a tie pin, we do not recommend adding a lapel pin; it will over-accessorize the look.

Groomsmen

If you have groomsmen, consider styling them in the same black suit with a plain white dress shirt and no necktie. Without the necktie, the groomsmen should unfasten the first two buttons of the dress shirt and make sure the collar ends fit nicely underneath the jacket lapel. If you prefer that the groomsmen wear a necktie, consider a neutral color that will complement the wedding color palette. Try to avoid deep colors that will take attention away from the bride and groom. You can add a small boutonnière to more easily distinguish the groomsmen from your wedding guests.

WHERE TO WEAR

The black suit is a great option for the Chic Groom. We recommend the following venue types:

- Chic indoor wedding: church, warehouse, restaurant, art museum, city hall, or historic home

- Chic outdoor wedding: historic inn, bed & breakfast, winery, or sculpture garden

WAYS TO SAVE

- Purchase a decorative pin that can be used as a tie pin or lapel pin long after the wedding. For extra savings, consider purchasing it from a vintage store or using a pin that may have been passed down from a family member.

- Tuxedo shirts can often be very expensive when purchased from high-end retailers. Save half the cost or more by purchasing it from a discount retailer that sells name brands.

THE GROOM IN COLOR

GET THE LOOK

Buttercream Notch Lapel Suit

Light Blue Oxford Shirt
with White Contrast Collar

Navy Silk Knit Tie

Vintage Gold Tie Clip

Gold Collar Pin

Silk Navy and White
Herringbone Pocket Square

Navy and Buttercream
Polka Dot Braces

Brown Leather Chukka Boots

Gold Link Wristwatch

Floral Boutonnière

THE GROOM IN COLOR

Do you remember when you were first introduced to color? Remember how excited you were to open that small box of eight crayons? It only included primary colors like blue, red, and yellow. As time progressed, you were introduced to the box of 64 crayons, and a whole new world opened. Even more excitement filled your eyes as you were able to color with peach, burnt sienna, and periwinkle. Since then, you've been hooked on color—the more vibrant and bold, the better.

The Groom in Color aims to be different through his use of color in his wardrobe, and most importantly, for his wedding day. He is artistic, confident, and adventurous, willing to travel off the beaten "black tuxedo" path.

This groom is wearing a buttercream notch lapel suit paired with a light blue, contrast collar, oxford shirt. The combination of buttercream and light blue makes for a great spring/summer look for the groom who does not want to wear a traditional look. A navy silk knit tie was used to anchor and formalize the look, since any other color tie might come across as too playful and distracting. The suit's color choice alone will have your guests in awe of your fashion sense and creativity.

Vintage finds were a key part of this look, as well. Some of the smaller styling pieces found at vintage stores added unique details. The gold collar pin, the gold tie clip, and the navy and buttercream polka dot braces were all vintage elements that really separate this look from that of the average groom. We finished it off with a dark brown leather chukka-style dress boot and a navy and white herringbone pocket square. When choosing a pocket square, we generally like to take cues from smaller details within a patterned tie. The key is to choose a color within the tie that is subtle; then, take that color, and make it the prominent color of your pocket square. If the tie is a solid color, there is a little more freedom. Selecting the same color or print of the tie for the pocket square may be too "matchy". We advise you choose this combination wisely.

Master the Details

Silk Knit Ties

Silk knit ties are an excellent way to introduce texture to your look. Silk knit gives you the combination of a formal look with the casual style of a knit tie. A solid color knit tie is highly encouraged for your wedding.

Tie Bar

Tie bars add a nice point of detail to your look. For many, tie bars serve a very functional purpose—to secure the tie in place. For others, they are added for styling purposes only. Either way, if you decide to wear one, make sure that it is placed on the tie between the third and fourth buttons from the top of the dress shirt.

Braces

Braces that clip on to pants tend to look a bit juvenile. Instead, go to a local tailor to have buttons added to the interior of your slacks for braces. It is a very simple detail, but you will be happy with the results. Wearing braces that are properly secured gives you a cleaner, more sophisticated look at your waistline without having to worry about a clasp popping off during the wedding festivities.

Pockets

On your wedding day, be mindful of things you place into your pant pockets like a cell phone, wallet, or mints. By putting things in your pockets, you run the risk of an unsightly bulge that can show up in your wedding photos. If you have to carry something, make sure it is properly stored in your jacket's interior pocket. Remind your groomsmen of this, as well.

Groomsmen

We suggest your groomsmen wear your same suit and knit tie. In lieu of the light blue oxford shirt with contrast collar, they can wear crisp white oxford shirts. That way, your light blue shirt will stand out and allow you to be the style star of the group.

WHERE TO WEAR

The buttercream suit is a great option for the Groom in Color. We recommend wearing it for one of the following venue types:

- Indoor wedding: a private residence, museum, city hall, finished barn, or restaurant
- Outdoor wedding: a historic inn, private residence, park, or sculpture garden

WAYS TO SAVE

- Shop for accoutrements at a vintage store or consignment shop. The printed braces, tie clip, and collar pin from this look were all vintage. Vintage items are often less expensive, and your rare finds will add character to your look.

GET THE LOOK

Blue Notch Lapel Suit
White Dress Shirt
Blue Silk Necktie
Silk Paisley Print Pocket Square
White Burlap Bloom Lapel Pin
Black Leather Lace-Up Boots
Navy Wool Pork Pie Fedora

In this look, we have the groom in a blue suit. A true blue will complement most bridal gowns and has been an increasingly popular color for grooms. Many businessmen choose navy blue suits for work, so we chose a shade lighter for the suit and paired it with a crisp white point collar dress shirt. A classic white shirt tends to work better for a look like this. By wearing a colored shirt, you run the risk of looking more like a businessman than a groom. To achieve a more formal look, we chose a tie in the same shade of blue as the suit. Silk and knit neckties or bow ties work well for this suit type. Also, we do not recommend choosing a blue suit with a ticket pocket. Ticket pockets were historically worn by businessmen—which we have established is not the look you want.

For detailing, a white burlap bloom lapel pin was added in place of a floral boutonnière. Make sure to choose a lapel pin that does not distract the eye from the rest of your look. To show some fun with the overall look, we added a multi-colored paisley silk pocket square, which incorporates the white and blue colors. The added accessories should work together to complement the look without standing out individually.

WHERE TO WEAR

The blue notch lapel suit is a great option for the Groom in Color. We recommend wearing it for one of the following venue types:

- Indoor wedding: a private residence, city hall, restaurant, historic cottage, or loft

- Outdoor wedding: a historic inn, private residence, vineyard, botanical garden, or stone barn

WAYS TO SAVE

- Purchase a blue suit in a lightweight wool material that can be worn year round. This material will allow you to wear the suit again following the wedding.

- Purchase a good quality pork pie fedora. A nice hat can be a statement piece for years to come.

Master the Details

Hats

Hats are a great way of showing off your style. A classic style like the pork pie fedora, also known as the "stingy brim," is a nice way to make your statement without being over the top. Make sure you choose a color that works well with your wedding look so that your accessory does not stick out like a sore thumb. Also, remember to wear the hat when it is appropriate. It should not be worn for your ceremony but could be a fun detail or prop during your wedding reception.

Lapel Pin

Keep this look simple with a bloom lapel pin. There are many different colors and shapes available to add to your lapel, but choose wisely. Take cues from your bride's bouquet, and only select a color displayed within her arrangement. There is no need to reinvent the wheel by choosing an arbitrary color.

Shoes

Your choice of footwear is very important while wearing a blue suit. The difference of wearing black or brown shoes can change your wedding look entirely. Black and blue combinations will generally lend itself to a more elegant look. Brown shoes can be considered more of a casual look. Wear black shoes if your venue is a bit more on the fancy side. Choose brown if you're getting married outside in a barn or in a field at a vineyard.

Groomsmen

Your groomsmen can wear the same suit and tie combination to show uniformity. As we have pointed out previously, it is important for the groom to stand out from his groomsmen, so have your guys wear white pocket squares with a simple square fold. You can also tone it down by not choosing a boutonnière for their looks. Instead, a gold or silver lapel pin could be a nice detail and a departure from the norm. You could even provide lapel pins as a part of their groomsmen gifts.

GET THE LOOK

Wintergreen Double-Breasted Suit

White Point Collar Dress Shirt

Tartan Plaid Bow Tie

Silk Black and White Houndstooth Pocket Square

Wintergreen Velvet Loafers

Wristwatch with Leather Band

Floral Boutonnière

This wintergreen double-breasted suit is a non-traditional spin on a traditional look. This look is for the groom who dances to the beat of his own drum. It is no surprise that he enjoys a splash of color in his wardrobe, and the same will be true for his wedding day. Yes, maybe you are not really the chapel kind of guy but would rather get married in a trendy outdoor space.

Often the double-breasted suit is viewed as formal attire due to the peak lapels and slimmer, more tailored cut. With this look, the green adds a bit of whimsy, throwing caution to the wind, while the peak lapels add elegance and regality. It's perfect for an intimate elopement or small wedding in a beautiful setting with those you love most.

To complete the double-breasted look, we added a crisp white dress shirt, tartan plaid bow tie, houndstooth pocket square, wintergreen velvet slippers, and a floral boutonnière to complement the bride's bouquet. We like the addition of the tartan plaid because it adds sophistication to the design of the double-breasted suit while maintaining the tone of a non-traditional look. Rather than selecting a necktie, which makes the look more business-like, we chose a classic bow tie to maintain formality. A necktie is not our style recommendation. However, if you decide to go with it, find one that is the same shade of green as the suit, or go with black. Any other colors can quickly go wrong, making you appear less than dapper.

Also, when wearing a double-breasted suit jacket, resist any temptation to wear the jacket unbuttoned. Different from a single-breasted suit that is typically unbuttoned when seated, the double-breasted suit should remain fastened at all times. If you must unfasten it to sit comfortably, remember to button the jacket when you stand again.

Master the Details

Suit Buttons

Generally, double-breasted suit jackets are made with either four or six buttons: two columns of two buttons or two columns of three buttons, respectively. There are workable buttons on the right column and non-workable ones on the left column. When wearing a suit jacket with four buttons, button the top workable button only. When wearing a suit jacket with six buttons, fasten the middle workable button only.

Pant Cuffs

Since your wedding look may veer on the non-traditional side, it may be a great detail to add a cuff to your pants anywhere from 1.25" to 1.5". Anything more runs the risk of being too trendy, or if you are a shorter groom, shortening your leg in proportion to the rest of your body.

Fit

Fit is particularly important when wearing a double-breasted suit. Wider lapels and extra buttons at the mid-section can have a widening effect to your shoulders and stomach area. Peak lapels work exceptionally well for slim builds, giving the appearance of broader shoulders and a slimmer waistline. If you are not going the custom-made route, consider hiring a tailor who can help you achieve the proper fit with an off-the-rack suit.

Velvet Loafers

If wintergreen shoes are just too much for you, consider wearing loafers in black velvet or black leather with this double-breasted look. You could wear a black leather lace-up, as well.

Groomsmen

Your groomsmen will be dapper in the same double-breasted suit in black. For uniformity, add the same tartan printed bow tie, houndstooth pocket square and velvet loafers in green. You will really emerge as the groom as your wintergreen suit becomes the focal point amongst your groomsmen. Your suits will be the same type, providing a very impactful, sartorial presence of debonair gentlemen.

WHERE TO WEAR

The wintergreen double-breasted suit is a great option for the Groom in Color. We recommend this fun look for the following venue types:

- Indoor wedding: a private residence, loft, theater, or distillery

- Outdoor wedding: a park, sculpture garden, European villa, grand tent, or private estate

WAYS TO SAVE

- Vintage stores are often a great source for finding plaid bow ties and neckties. Because some plaids are timeless in their appearance, a vintage plaid bow tie can look as current as a newly purchased bow tie.

- Shop for a good quality white point collar shirt at a local discount retailer rather than a larger famous retailer. You will save considerably.

THE PREPPY GROOM

GET THE LOOK

Madras Plaid Sport Coat

White Club Collar Dress Shirt

Ecru Chino Pants

Navy Knit Tie

Navy Knit Bloom Lapel Pin

Gold Safety-Pin Style Collar Pin

White Gauze Pocket Square

Blue Rope Bracelet with
Leather Accents

Brown Saddle Oxford Shoes

THE PREPPY GROOM

If you're preppy, and you know it, clap your hands! This look is for the guy who is preppy yet confident. When we think of a preppy groom, we think of the guy who has, or desires to have, a very collegiate look—one who looks as if he has just stepped off an Ivy League campus. He was possibly a debate team captain, a rugby or lacrosse player, or maybe even a student body president. This groom's style is reminiscent of the classic film, *Dead Poets Society*, or the '80s comedy, *Making the Grade*.

LOOK ONE

The sport coat shown here is in madras plaid, which is a traditional preppy plaid. We paired the sport coat, which serves as a statement piece, with the muted color ecru in the chino pants. This pairing keeps the look clean and simple. We also chose a club collar shirt, which is a very preppy choice. A navy knit tie and a rope bracelet introduce nautical elements for this wedding near the dock. Due to the look's casual nature, we opted to omit dress socks and gave a messy roll to the pants. If you decide to give madras a try, don't feel that you have to wear an entire suit of it. It could be way too much plaid. Besides, your bride should be the focal point—not your suit.

Before selecting this look for your wedding day, consult with your bride and your stylist to make sure that it would be appropriate for your wedding in terms of formality. As noted, this look is on the casual side; however, it may work for a semi-formal wedding or elopement. If your wedding is very formal, consider this look for a preppy-style rehearsal dinner or post-wedding brunch.

Master the Details

Mixing Plaids

Do not mix plaids. For your wedding day, we do not recommend mixing a plaid shirt or plaid slacks with the madras sport coat. Keep it simple with a neutral dress shirt and slacks.

Socks

Skip the socks, and give your pants a messy roll.

Pocket Square

Consider a three-point fold for your pocket square, shown in this look. The three-point, pocket square fold can be used in more casual looks.

Fit

Make sure that the sport coat fits well throughout. If the sport coat is too small in the shoulders or biceps, it will be more noticeable in a madras plaid than in a black suit or tuxedo jacket due to the material's pattern.

Boutonnière

Due to the complexity of the madras plaid, it may be good to skip the floral boutonnière and opt for a lapel pin in a solid color.

Groomsmen

Leave this statement sport coat for the groom only, and select a complementary look for the groomsmen. One option is to pair the groom's same ecru chino pants with navy cotton waistcoats, white dress shirts, and navy cotton neckties or bow ties.

WHERE TO WEAR

The madras sport coat should be worn at a wedding that is more preppy in nature, and most definitely in a warmer climate. We recommend the following venue types:

- Preppy indoor wedding: yacht club, country club, or inn

- Preppy outdoor wedding: lake, boathouse, dock, or grand tent

WAYS TO SAVE

- Purchase a medium weight, chino pant that can be worn for years to come. Chinos tend to be long lasting—getting better with age. They can even be cut into shorts.

- Purchase a knit bloom lapel pin that can be worn again.

- Skip the cufflinks. Many cotton club collar shirts are available with standard buttons at the sleeves and do not require cufflinks.

GET THE LOOK

Blue and White Pincord
Slim Fit Suit

Light Pink Oxford Shirt with
Button-Down Collar

Repp Tie with Navy and Kelly
Green Stripes

Silver Safety-Pin Style Collar Pin

Silver Tie Bar

White Cotton Pocket Square

Silver Link Wristwatch

Wooden Bracelets

Brown Leather Derby Shoes

Floral Boutonniere

LOOK TWO

The pincord suit is a versatile option for the preppy groom. It can transition easily from a semi-formal wedding at a church to an outdoor or beachside reception. Keep in mind that a pincord suit is seasonal and should be worn only for a warm weather wedding. An alternative for a spring or summer preppy wedding is a seersucker suit.

We paired this lightweight blue and white pincord suit with a pastel pink oxford shirt. Instead of the pastel pink, you could also wear a canary yellow shirt with a similar suit. To give a more preppy vibe, we added a navy and green repp tie for pattern-play. If this is too much for you, go with a solid necktie in navy or bright green. We also featured the pincord suit with a more subdued but equally formal option, using a solid navy diamond tip bow tie. It is a more simplistic approach to the preppy attire, but the minor adjustment changes the outfit's look and feel.

For shoe options, a simple derby or blucher shoe helps to balance the overall look. Since the wedding suit is non-traditional, choosing a derby or blucher shoe will bring back a bit of traditionalism to the look. We advise staying away from a sneaker with this suit. Here, we have selected a dark brown derby shoe, as it pairs well with the pastel colors of the suit and dress shirt. As a final touch, add a simple white pocket square with a straight fold. It will keep the look clean and will not compete with the floral boutonnière.

Master the Details

Mixing Pincords

Do not mix different pincords. If you choose to purchase only the pincord jacket or the pincord pants, make sure that the other half of the pair is solid. Do not mix pincord pieces in different colors.

Collar Pin

A safety-pin style, collar pin is a nice element to add to a preppy look. Not only is it functional, to keep the shirt collar ends in place, but it also allows the necktie to sit up a little bit higher for an added air of sophistication. When pairing the collar pin with a button-down collar shirt, consider keeping the collar buttons unfastened when the collar pin is in place.

Socks

Skip the socks. Because a pincord suit is more fitting for a wedding in a warmer climate, socks are not necessary. If you opt for socks with this look, make sure that the socks complement your shoe choice and the striped pattern of the suit.

Boutonnière

Consider a single flower boutonnière or no boutonnière at all. If you choose a single flower, our preference is for it to be small or a bud. It should be a subtle accent to the look, not a focal point. The boutonnière should be placed on the left lapel of the jacket, covering the buttonhole on the lapel.

Groomsmen

You can style the groomsmen in the same suit pants. In lieu of the suit jacket, opt for waistcoats in the matching pincord material. This will easily identify you as the groom and the others as your attendants.

WHERE TO WEAR

The pincord suit should be worn at a wedding that is more preppy in nature, and definitely in a warmer climate. We recommend the following venue types:

- Preppy indoor wedding: church, historical home or manor, resort, or inn

- Preppy outdoor wedding: beach or grand tent

WAYS TO SAVE

- Purchase an oxford shirt in lieu of a tuxedo shirt, since oxford shirts are typically less expensive.

- Purchase a plain white handkerchief or pocket square. Plain white cotton pocket squares are a great, and often less expensive, alternative to pocket squares in other fabrics, colors, and patterns.

- Skip the cufflinks. Most oxford shirts come with standard buttons at the sleeves, so cufflinks are not required for this look.

GET THE LOOK (option)

In lieu of the repp tie, collar pin, and tie bar shown previously, a navy blue diamond tip bow tie can be used to complete this look rather nicely. The solid bow tie is a bit simpler, and may be better for a groom who prefers to wear a bow tie on his wedding day.

In this option, we have also eliminated the boutonnière for a cleaner look. If you prefer not to wear a boutonnière, then skip it.

GET THE LOOK

Navy Blazer with Gold Buttons and Notch Lapel

White Spread Collar Dress Shirt

White Cotton Blend Shorts

Navy and Ivory Basket Weave Print Tie

White Cotton Pocket Square

Brown Leather Square Buckle Belt

White Buck (Oxford) Shoes

Floral Boutonnière

LOOK THREE

The navy blazer with gold buttons is one of the staple pieces in a preppy man's wardrobe. It is a classic and versatile piece that adds distinction to just about any preppy outfit. A well-tailored navy blazer can be worn year after year without going out of style. We have paired the navy blazer with non-traditional elements in this section. You may find that these looks are a little too non-traditional for your wedding day, but may be great options for your rehearsal dinner or other wedding weekend activities.

In this look, the navy blazer is styled with a dress shirt, necktie, and white shorts. We bet you never considered wearing shorts and a navy blazer to your wedding. It is a bit unexpected and unique, but could be quite appropriate depending on your wedding theme and venue.

As with any wedding day look, you must make sure that you are matching the level of formality of your bride's dress. We specifically say "dress" here and not gown. If your bride is wearing a full-length formal gown for your wedding, this is not the look for you. This groom's look is suited for a more informal wedding, where the bride may be wearing a simple sheath dress or an A-line tea length dress. She does not have to give away all of the details of her dress before the wedding day, but be sure to consult with her about your decision to wear shorts. If she is opposed to it, please, don't do it. Save this look for another occasion. Remember guys—happy wife, happy life. Now, if you both decide that it is, indeed, a good look for your wedding day, throw caution to the wind, and rock this look the best you can!

Master the Details

Fit
When selecting shorts for your wedding day, fit is critical. Shorts that are too long or too short can ruin the whole look. Opt for a classic fit pair of shorts that hit right above your knees. This will likely be a pair of shorts with a 9" to 10.5" inseam, depending on the length of your legs. Also, classic fit shorts will provide a more appropriate look than slim fit shorts.

Legs
If you decide to go the shorts route, make sure that you do not have chicken legs in your wedding photos. Do calf raises at the gym to make sure that your legs look their best while on display.

Socks
Lose the socks for this look. Adding socks will give the outfit an athletic appearance, and that's not the look we are going for.

Pocket Square
A puff fold is a great option for this look, since it is more casual. The puff fold helps tie in the semi-formal elements of the navy blazer with the casual white shorts.

Groomsmen
Consider styling the groomsmen in the same look as the groom. To distinguish yourself from your attendants, wear a different tie or boutonnière.

WHERE TO WEAR
The navy blazer paired with shorts should be worn at a preppy outdoor wedding. This look most certainly should be in a warmer climate. We recommend the following venue types:

- Preppy outdoor wedding: beach, park, lake, boathouse, or inn

WAYS TO SAVE
- Purchase a navy blazer with gold buttons that can be worn year after year following the wedding.
- Purchase classic fit shorts in lieu of more costly dress slacks.

GET THE LOOK

Navy Blazer with Gold Buttons and Notch Lapel

Blue and White Bengal Striped Shirt with Button-Down Collar

Navy and Gold Repp Tie

White Cotton Pocket Square with Navy Trim

Vintage Gold Tie Bar

Nantucket Red Chino Pants

Green and Cream Ribbon Belt

Saddle Oxford Shoes

LOOK FOUR

We also provided another option for wearing a classic navy blazer. This time we styled the blazer more on the conservative side, but it is still very true to its preppy roots. Either way, you are guaranteed to look proper and collegiate, and overall, smartly dressed.

We paired the navy blazer with Nantucket red chinos. Do not be alarmed by the color. Many guys are not comfortable wearing this shade of red, so you could opt for a chino in grass green, bright or canary yellow, orange, or in some instances blue—shy away from navy. Pairing navy chinos with a navy blazer tends to look like a mismatched suit. It may appear that you were too cheap to buy a full navy suit. If you decide on blue, you should try wearing a different shade. Go for sky blue, aquamarine, royal blue, or cobalt. However, if all of this color is too much, you could select a khaki or sand-colored chino instead.

This groom is also wearing a white button-down shirt with blue Bengal stripes. In order to add a bit more "prep" to this mix, we chose a blue and gold collegiate repp tie and a green and white striped ribbon belt. The repp tie is one of the many quintessential ties for a preppy guy and is sold in a variety of bold colors. For footwear, we added a saddle oxford shoe, which has been a prep school staple for years. For finishing touches, we chose a tie clip to keep the tie in place and to add character, along with wooden bracelets. Set no limits aside from looking appropriate for your wedding and your bride.

Master the Details

Socks

Skip the socks, altogether, with this look. As a Preppy Groom, you will be getting married in a warmer climate, most likely, where socks are not necessary. Besides, you have enough going on with your look without socks being another focal point.

Pant Style

Select a flat front pant. They are a great option for the modern groom and can be found in a variety of colors and fabrics. When tailored appropriately, they have a slimming effect.

Color

The Preppy Groom has a playful vibe. Pops of color here and there will work well for this look. Incorporate color as much as possible, within reason. The navy blazer anchors the look and keeps it from looking too busy.

Fit

Remember to maintain the appropriate size relationship between your blazer and your pants. Essentially, they are considered separates because they are not a full suit. Therefore, if your blazer is slim and tailored, your chinos should be the same.

Groomsmen

Consider styling the groomsmen in the same navy blazer, dress shirt, and tie. In place of the Nantucket red pants, the groomsmen could wear khaki chinos, making the groom easily identifiable.

WHERE TO WEAR

The navy blazer paired with Nantucket red pants should be worn for a preppy wedding in a warmer climate. We recommend the following venue types:

- Preppy indoor wedding: country club, social club, inn, or historic New England-style church
- Preppy outdoor wedding: country club, social club, inn, or boathouse

WAYS TO SAVE

- Purchase a navy blazer with gold buttons that can be worn year after year following the wedding.
- Skip the boutonnière. With the mix of patterns and colors in this look, it is unnecessary and could be more of a distraction, overall.

GET THE LOOK

White Linen Blend Slim Fit Blazer with a Notched Lapel

Blue and White Bengal Striped Spread Collar Shirt

Navy and White Polka Dot Tie

Vintage Gold Tie Bar

Navy and White Herringbone Plaid Pocket Square

Navy Slim Fit Slacks

Black Leather Cap Toe Boot

Wooden Bracelets

Floral Boutonnière

LOOK FIVE

There is just something special about a white blazer. The color alone is crisp, clean, and fresh. Paired with a darker pant, you will look stylish and very distinguished, giving you another perfect option for an outdoor or indoor wedding. This is for a sophisticated groom who wants to achieve an elegant look in a non-traditional way. White and navy are the basis of this look and have been selected for the suit separates. We selected a lighter color on top and a darker color on the bottom; most often, you see the opposite. As a complement to the suit separates, we played with a mix of patterns for the dress shirt, tie, and pocket square in the same colors of navy and white. Playing with patterns can be a bit tricky, but when done correctly, it adds detail to your look. The key is to choose patterns with a very simple print. You want to make sure that your pattern play is sharp, but not so bold that you draw attention away from your bride. The navy and white colors make the look a bit nautical in theme, which makes it a great option for a wedding on a yacht.

If you are the clumsy type who will spill your drink or food on yourself, we suggest that you take the jacket off during the meal. It has to be clean and well-kept, so no rough-and-tumble activity, sir!

Master the Details

Spread Collar Shirt

A spread collar shirt provides a more classic look than a point collar or button-down collar shirt.

Necktie Length

As a general rule, the tip of the tie should fall just below the top of the waistband of your pants when you are standing straight. It may take a couple times to do it correctly, but it is worth the time spent to get it right.

Pant Break

Check your breaks! The break in your pant refers to the amount of fabric that creases at the bottom of your pant in relation to your shoes. There are a few options with pant breaks: no break, half break, and full break. For a slimmer pant, we prefer no break as shown in this look. Pooling fabric around your ankles can be unsightly and change your entire look.

Boutonnière

To give a small pop to the look, select flowers that are different colors than the color palette of your outfit, but still within the color theme of your wedding. We recommend a single flower as the focus. Less is more when it comes to boutonnières.

Groomsmen

Consider styling the groomsmen in full navy suits with the same fit as the groom's suit separates. For a less formal look, style the groomsmen in navy waistcoats with matching slacks. To keep the attention on the groom's look, the groomsmen can be styled in white dress shirts with solid ties.

WHERE TO WEAR

This suit-separates look should be worn at a wedding with a slight preppy but elegant flair. It is suitable for a warmer climate, but could be worn for a traditional fall weather wedding, as well. We recommend the following venue types:

- Preppy but elegant indoor wedding: church, mansion, country club, social club, or old English-style inn

- Preppy but elegant outdoor wedding: mansion, country club, social club, old English-style inn, vineyard, or yacht

WAYS TO SAVE

- Purchase a cap toe leather boot. It is a good shoe option that can be worn year-round after the wedding is done.

- A spread collar shirt makes a very strong statement by itself and does not require the purchase of a collar bar or collar pin.

THE
RUSTIC
GROOM

GET THE LOOK

Chambray Shirt with
Button-Down Collar

Denim Waistcoat

Denim Necktie

White Bronze Arrowhead
Necklace

Silver Safety-Pin Style Collar Pin

Workman Jeans

Southwestern Leather Belt

Brown Suede Engineer Boots

Wooden Bracelets

Sterling Silver Cuff with
Turquoise Inlay

THE RUSTIC GROOM

Open fields, farms, and desert lands are the places that inspire the Rustic Groom. You'll find him admiring mountain views, billowing trees, and anything else related to nature. The Rustic Groom is earthy and unpretentious—lending himself to the beauty of nature and his surroundings, along with all the fresh air Mother Nature has to offer. This guy is practical and would much rather spend his time basking in the country sunshine with the love of his life without a worry of refinement. He is outdoorsy and adventurous, living in his jeans. For all you "no fuss, no frills" types who refuse to wear a suit or tuxedo, there are other options. It's okay. You don't have to wear anything you don't want to. This is your special day, too, and you should look and feel comfortable.

With all its many shades, rinses, fits, weights, and types, denim is a great option for the Rustic Groom. Since there are a number of options out there, it is important that you choose wisely. For this groom, we chose a medium-rinse denim that complements his bride's lighter blue chambray blouse.

In order to achieve a cleaner look with jeans, consider trying a denim or chambray shirt. This pairing is affectionately known as a Canadian Tuxedo. It is when a denim or chambray shirt or jacket are styled with similarly colored jeans. Now, don't choose any old denim shirt; it has to be one that makes sense. To elevate the look, we added a denim waistcoat, which gives it a more formal feel.

The key to making this look work is fit, since it is not a traditional, tailored suit. Because you are trying to create a certain level of formality with casual elements, choose items that are appropriate to your physique and not too baggy. Remember, if the fit is off, the whole look will be off.

Another element that works well is the use of earth-tone accents in this look. Since this groom is a bit more grass roots, rich tones of amber, brown, green, and tan would be perfect for him. If you are gravitating towards this look for your wedding, consider adding these colors within your shoe selection or accessories to help accentuate the denim-on-denim look.

The accessories for this look include a denim necktie, a collar pin, a Southwestern-inspired vintage leather belt, and a white bronze arrowhead necklace. Accessories are key to an overall look, especially if your look is non-traditional. Have fun with your accessory selection; just remember, it's all in the details, my friends. Style is all in the details.

Master the Details

Sleeves

With this non-traditional wedding look, it is really important that you look and feel comfortable in your outfit choice. Consider giving a messy roll to the sleeves. Don't stop at the forearms; keep rolling to just below your elbow.

Buttons

When wearing a waistcoat, the proper etiquette is to leave the last button unfastened.

Boots

Unlike a classic wedding look, for which we encourage grooms to purchase a brand new pair of shoes for the wedding day, the Rustic Groom can get away with a stylish pair of worn-in engineer boots. They should be worn in, but not so much that they have holes or that the soles are coming off.

Accessories

To make this look appear authentic, do not overdo it with accessories. Choose a mixture of contemporary and vintage items that help you truly embody the essence of the Rustic Groom.

Fit

If the denim shirt that you select is a little large in the body, consider taking it to your local tailor to have it slimmed down. This will ensure a better fit with the waistcoat.

Boutonnière

We typically prefer a rustic waistcoat look without a boutonnière. However, if you feel that it is essential, consider selecting a small one that is inspired by the surroundings of your rustic wedding.

Groomsmen

Consider styling the groomsmen in jeans and the same waistcoat. You may select a different button down shirt in white or cream, and possibly omit the necktie. Also, the groomsmen should not have as many accessories. As the groom, you should shine with your rustic, vintage jewelry and accoutrements.

WHERE TO WEAR

This denim-on-denim look is for a wedding with a rustic flair. We recommend the following venue types:

- Rustic indoor wedding: barn, mountain club, or lodge

- Rustic outdoor wedding: farm, ranch, park, or desert

WAYS TO SAVE

- Purchase accessories for your rustic look from a thrift store or vintage shop.

- Wear a pair of broken-in jeans that you may already have in your closet.

- Wear a pair of engineer boots that you already own.

GET THE LOOK

Tan Corduroy Sport Coat

Chambray Button-Down Shirt

Wool Herringbone Plaid Tie

Silver Safety-Pin Style Collar Pin

Saddle Leather Bloom Lapel Pin

Wooden Bracelets

Navy Bandana
(as a Pocket Square)

Dark Rinse Jeans

Tan Suede Chelsea Boots

Inspired by the colors and textures of the harvest season for this groom, we kept the denim-on-denim inspiration but switched it up with contrasting shades of denim and the addition of a wide wale corduroy sport coat. It is a perfect look for a more casual wedding taking place in a barn, on a ranch, or at a farmhouse with a naturally beautiful backdrop of haystacks, rolling hills, and agriculture. Perfect for the fall wedding, this look will draw out the rich autumnal shades of burnt orange, reds, and yellow—like the changing leaves.

To add some interesting features, we selected a safety-pin style collar pin, leather bloom lapel pin, wooden bracelets, and suede Chelsea boots. You could also substitute the chambray shirt for a clean, white or cream button-down shirt. Ditch your traditional pocket square, and use a bandana.

There is one pitfall that you want to avoid when selecting the jacket for this look, since every jacket is not the same. Instead of a suit jacket, we have selected a corduroy sport coat. Many gentlemen make the mistake of pairing a suit jacket with jeans, which often times ends up looking quite strange. Suit jackets, in most instances, are more fitted and are not intended to be worn separately from their matching pants. Sport coats are typically looser in fit, which is appropriate for layering with a sweater or vest, and are often made of durable material. In addition to the corduroy, our sport coat has brown suede patches on the elbow and pockets, which is not typically found on suit jackets. The patch pockets have been sewn to the outside of the jacket, while most suit jackets have pockets sewn inside the interior.

With a rustic look similar to this, remember to always factor your wedding location and venue when selecting your wardrobe. Many grooms do not think outside the box with their wedding day look and quickly opt for a formal black tuxedo. There are many other options available that will still allow you to look amazing. If your bride opts for a short lace sheath dress instead of a formal gown, this just might be the look for you. If you love the look but decide that it just will not work for your wedding day, consider it for a rustic or farm-inspired rehearsal dinner.

Master the Details

Jeans
Different from the previous Rustic Groom look, a pair of worn out, faded jeans just will not do. A new, or gently used, pair of jeans will be better suited for this look since they will be paired with a sport coat and Chelsea boots. The new jeans may not be as comfortable as the ones you have had for two years, but they certainly will look cleaner and more appropriate for your wedding day. Make sure that they are a classic fit, not too slim or baggy.

Pocket Square
Use a bandana as a pocket square. It is completely unexpected but totally appropriate for the Rustic Groom. If you find the bandana to be too large, just cut it in half to reduce its bulkiness.

Collar Pin
A safety-pin style collar pin is appropriate for this groom because it adds a bit of traditional detailing to an unconventional look. Functionally, it helps to keep the tie knot in place and secure your shirt collar from shifting. For color consistency, choose a gold or bronze pin.

Boots
Chelsea boots are amazing, in general. They are first-rate among classic shoe options, without the fuss of laces. A suede Chelsea boot provides just enough refinement for a wedding day look but also gives the look a bit of that rugged sensibility you embody.

Boutonnière
If you prefer something different from the traditional floral boutonnière, try a leather bloom lapel pin in tan, which will help tie the look together. It is quick and easy, and most importantly, you can wear it again and again.

Groomsmen
Style your groomsmen in the same chambray button-down shirt and jeans. In lieu of the corduroy sport coat, consider adding braided leather braces to their shirts and jeans.

WHERE TO WEAR

The corduroy sport coat and denim look is for a harvest season wedding with a rustic flair. We recommend the following venue types:

- Rustic indoor wedding: barn, mountain club, or lodge
- Rustic outdoor wedding: farm, ranch, or park

WAYS TO SAVE

- Purchase a timeless, but rugged sport coat that can be used often after the wedding.
- Purchase a pair of inexpensive dark rinse jeans. Jeans should result in considerable savings from the purchase of suit pants or dress slacks.
- Purchase a navy bandana to use as a pocket square.

THE ISLAND GROOM

GET THE LOOK

Ivory Linen-Blend Blazer

White Dress Shirt

White Slim Fit Chinos

Bloom Lapel Pin in Nude

Wooden Bracelets

White Espadrilles

White Panama Hat

THE ISLAND GROOM

Calm. Cool. Collected. Caribbean? Let's travel away for a bit with our Island Groom who is ready to say "I do" amidst the tropical breeze. If this is you, you will want to keep it simple and clean—perhaps you should leave the tuxedo or business suit at home. Celebrate your island wedding in a style that is comfortable and casual but appropriate for your nuptials.

This non-traditional groom is wearing a cream-colored, two-button notch lapel blazer in a lightweight cotton-linen blend material—very breathable for the warmer climate. We paired the blazer with a white dress shirt and white chinos, also in breathable cotton to keep him cool. Some people might not think white and cream would work well together. However, by making the cream blazer the feature element and the white shirt and pants the complementary pieces, this blazer is perfectly suitable for a ceremony on the beach. You could also select a white suit with a cream dress shirt. We typically try to stick with a 2:1 ratio when working with separates in neutral colors. In the case of a white suit, you would pair two items in white (the suit) with one item in cream (the dress shirt). Alternatively, you could pair a cream suit with a white dress shirt. Whichever way you choose, it is a perfect formula that works like a dream.

Footwear is very important for an island wedding. Your shoe choice could make or break your look. Because they are comfortable, beach-friendly, and inexpensive, we chose white espadrilles for this look. Your shoe selection has to make sense with the outfit. You could wear a leather brogue or wingtip, but does it really fit your ceremony or reception venues? What if your shoes get wet? Will the sand or stones from the beach ruin the leather? These are all legitimate questions, especially if you are exchanging vows right on the beach. If you want something a little more formal than an espadrille, a leather sandal or a huarache is another option. For the Island Groom, we recommend that you avoid wearing flip-flops with a blazer or suit. Only select flip-flops for a very casual outfit—possibly a linen shirt and pants. If you are going to wear flip-flops, opt for a leather version in lieu of rubber. It's your wedding day; don't cheapen your look with cheap-looking shoes.

To further accessorize the look, add a group of colorful wooden bracelets, as shown. You can play around with subtle tribal jewelry, but, as always, be careful not to overdo it. Remember, your bride is the focus, not your cool trinkets and doodads. A hat is also a great accessory for the Island Groom. In particular, a Panama hat is an excellent option because it is lightweight and perfect for warmer climates. It can easily be paired with a suit or suit separates and would be appropriate for the Island Groom.

Master the Details

Neckties

If your island wedding is more casual in nature, consider styling your look without a tie and unbuttoning the top two buttons of the shirt for a relaxed and carefree look. If you prefer to wear a tie, the correct way is to tighten it, so the top button of your dress shirt is covered. Because your wedding is in a warmer climate, be sure to resist the temptation to wear a loose tie with the top button unfastened.

Waistcoat

If the blazer is too formal for your island look, you can replace it with a cream waistcoat, similar to the material of your slacks. With the waistcoat, try rolling up the shirt sleeves for a more relaxed look.

Socks

We advise skipping the socks with this look. As an Island Groom, you will be getting married in a warmer climate and possibly on a beach where socks won't be necessary.

Hats

If you choose to wear a hat, save it for either your wedding photo session before or after the ceremony, or your reception, if it is outdoors. Be sure to remove the hat during the formal parts of your wedding day, including the ceremony, first dance, parents' dances, and dinner.

Sunglasses

Avoid wearing sunglasses during your wedding ceremony and reception, even in sunny weather. Your bride and your guests want to see your eyes to connect with you, not your Ray-Bans.

Groomsmen

Consider styling the groomsmen in the same dress shirt, slacks, and belt, but without the blazer. If you find the look to be too casual, add waistcoats to their look in a similar color to your blazer. We are not fans of adding boutonnières to dress shirts worn alone. However, a small floral boutonnière should work fine on waistcoats.

WHERE TO WEAR

This look should be worn for an island or warm weather wedding. We recommend the following venue types:

- Island-themed indoor wedding: church, beach club, resort, European villa, or island home

- Island-themed outdoor wedding: beach, resort, European villa, or island home

WAYS TO SAVE

- Purchase a pair of white espadrilles or leather Mexican huaraches, in lieu of dress shoes. A nice pair of espadrilles can be purchased for about fifty dollars, but a good pair of dress shoes can be up to four times as much.

- Authentic Panama hats can be expensive. Save half or more of the cost by purchasing a less expensive duplicate from a contemporary fashion retailer.

THE HOLIDAY GROOM

GET THE LOOK

Garnet Velvet Blazer
White Tuxedo Shirt
Black Silk Self-Tie Bow Tie
Black Tuxedo Pants
Black Leather Lace-Up Shoes
Black Silk Knot Cuff Links
Black Silk Knot Stud Set
White Cotton Pocket Square
Fabric Flower Lapel Pin

THE HOLIDAY GROOM

Something about the holiday season warms the heart. Perhaps, it is the combination of various things, like the smell of chestnuts roasting on an open fire, the cheerful carolers, the sacred lighting of Kwanzaa and menorah candles, and the magical Christmas lights strung from branch to branch. The winter months incite warm and cozy vibes, as many of us gather around a fireplace with friends and family.

As you find yourself getting endless invitations to holiday parties, we know you will not run out of ideas or inspiration on what to wear, especially if it is your own holiday wedding. It's no secret that a lot of couples get married during the holidays. For the Holiday Groom, you have a particularly festive style that is inspired by texture and warm, rich jewel tones that personify the beauty of the holiday season.

Cranberry or garnet colors often make people think of the holidays. Imagine standing before your beautiful bride while wearing a cranberry velvet blazer. She will be captivated, with her attention solely on you. For this look, we selected a bolder color for the blazer while keeping the other elements traditional. Wearing cranberry for your wedding can be tricky; however, here, we show you how to do it in an inconspicuous way, saving the attention for your bride. Wearing a bold color looks great, especially when you choose the right shade. Remember to carefully choose a color that is suitable for your skin tone, hair color, and wedding décor or theme.

For this look, we chose a cranberry or garnet velvet blazer, pairing it with traditional black and white. Since the blazer is the standout piece,

we kept everything else simple. Although the blazer is not a tuxedo jacket, we styled it with a white tuxedo shirt, black tuxedo pants, and black calf-skin, lace-up shoes to replicate the formality of a tuxedo. The finishing accoutrements include a black silk bow tie, black silk knot cufflinks, black silk knot studs, a white pocket square, and black socks. To decorate the lapel of the jacket, we gave a few options: a lapel flower pin made from black and white plaid fabric or a floral boutonnière. Both options will work; it is just a matter of preference.

As a gentleman and groom of style, remember, the lady is the primary focus. Choosing the right colors to wear is imperative; we cannot stress this enough. Be aware of the goal—that you both look like one.

Master the Details

Color

One of the keys to mastering this look is color choice. Jewel tones are great for holiday weddings. If garnet is not for you, consider other velvet blazers in jewel tones such as: emerald green, amethyst, topaz, or sapphire. All other elements (tuxedo shirt, tuxedo pants, shoes, etc.) of the look should remain the same; just swap the blazer for a color that is better suited for you.

Texture

Textured blazers are a great, festive choice for the Holiday Groom. Here, we selected velvet, but there are other options that are suitable for the winter and holiday seasons. Whether your blazer is velvet, doeskin, jacquard, pique, or something else, you'll definitely make a fashion statement that will be admired by your bride and wedding guests.

Fit

Fit is a major factor when considering any look, especially if you are wearing a bold colored blazer. You can get away with a lot with dark colors; however, when dealing with bright colors, you have less of a margin of error. Make sure your look fits impeccably or people will immediately notice that you did not nail it.

Groomsmen

For this look, your groomsmen should wear black tuxedos with the same lapel profile as your velvet blazer. Keep the cranberry blazer as a feature for the groom only. As a sign of uniformity, you could select the same floral boutonnière or lapel pin for you and your groomsmen.

WHERE TO WEAR

The garnet velvet blazer is most appropriate for a wedding during the holiday season. We recommend the following venue types:

- Formal indoor wedding: church, hotel ballroom, restaurant, resort lodge, cabin, theater, or art gallery

- Formal outdoor wedding: historic home or resort lodge

WAYS TO SAVE

- The silk knot cuff links and stud set are a nice complement to the velvet jacket. In addition, they are less expensive than other stud sets and cuff links.

- Purchase a good quality velvet blazer from a contemporary retailer, and have a tailor alter it to fit like it is custom-made.

GET THE LOOK

Sapphire Velvet Peak Lapel
Tuxedo Jacket

Black Flat Front Tuxedo Pants

White Tuxedo Shirt

Black Self-Tie Bow Tie

Black Dress Sock

Black Leather Lace-Up Shoes

Wristwatch with Leather Band

Floral Boutonnière

LOOK TWO

Velvet is a winner during the winter. It not only keeps you warm but also is debonair. This sapphire velvet tuxedo jacket with black satin lapels is a great choice for a formal evening wedding. The phrase "black tie" typically means wearing a black tuxedo and black bow tie, along with the whole classic tuxedo regalia. This look is not exactly black tie, but it does achieve an equal level of refinement. By wearing sapphire or navy, you can easily differentiate yourself from your attendants and guests while also coordinating with the many bridal gown options. It is a subtle departure from the black tie rules but very appropriate for a modern gentleman. This jacket is versatile and can be dressed up or down for you to wear again after your wedding day.

With the tuxedo jacket, we chose a classic white tuxedo shirt, black tuxedo pants, and black shoes to complement the black satin lapels of the jacket. Remember, you are at a formal event, which calls for more conservative dress. This is not the time to wear your black and white Chuck Taylor Converse or other wild shoe selections. Keep it classy for the holidays.

WHERE TO WEAR

The sapphire velvet tuxedo look is appropriate for a very formal, fashion-forward wedding during the holiday season. We recommend the following venue types:

- Formal indoor wedding: church, hotel ballroom, grand library, loft, or winery

- Formal outdoor wedding: vineyard or winery

WAYS TO SAVE

- Save the cost of purchasing cufflinks and a stud set by opting for a tuxedo shirt with plain buttons that does not require studs and cufflinks.

- For this look, you can eliminate the pocket square for a small savings.

Master the Details

Buttons

If your off-the-rack jacket comes with plastic buttons, consider having them switched out for fabric ones in the color and material of your jacket. Alternatively, exchange satin buttons to match the lapel of the jacket, if it is a tuxedo. Your local tailor should be able to assist you with changing out the buttons. You will see how something so minor can change or improve your look in a major way.

Peak Lapel

There are a few options when it comes to selecting the lapel profile for your suit or tuxedo jacket: notch, shawl, and peak. This look's lapel type is peak. The peak lapel is a very smart choice for this holiday groom. It is typically the most formal lapel type, so it matches well with the plush velvet material while providing a sense of edge or fashion-forwardness.

Pocket Square

For this look, we excluded the pocket square. Unlike the complementary look of a single flower or bud, the larger floral boutonnière shown would make for competing focal points with the pocket square. Remember, you have to have one place to attract the eye's attention.

Wristwatch

There are conflicting opinions on whether wristwatches are appropriate with tuxedos. In our opinion, they are fine to wear; however, as with all accoutrements, you must select wisely. For wedding apparel, including tuxedos, we prefer simple, elegant watches with faces appropriately sized to your wrist. The watch bands can be made of metal links or leather.

Groomsmen

Similar to the garnet velvet blazer, we recommend that the groomsmen wear classic black tuxedos with your same lapel profile, along with black bow ties. In this case, the groomsmen would wear peak lapel tuxedo jackets. For the attendants, you can choose a simpler floral boutonnière, and let yours be a bit fancier.

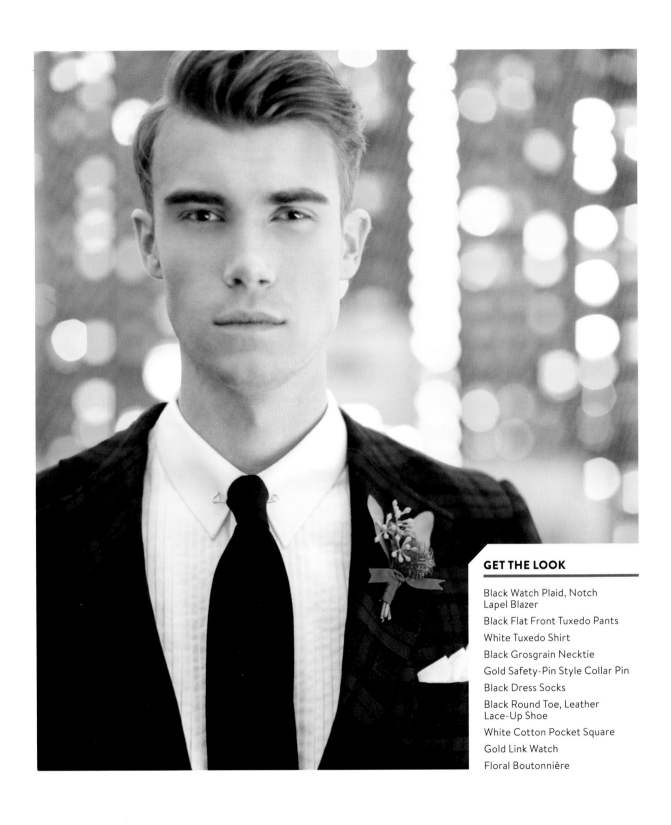

GET THE LOOK

Black Watch Plaid, Notch Lapel Blazer

Black Flat Front Tuxedo Pants

White Tuxedo Shirt

Black Grosgrain Necktie

Gold Safety-Pin Style Collar Pin

Black Dress Socks

Black Round Toe, Leather Lace-Up Shoe

White Cotton Pocket Square

Gold Link Watch

Floral Boutonnière

LOOK THREE

Black Watch tartan plaid is classic and has been around for ages. It is one of the most recognizable patterns in fashion. If you can envision yourself wearing a jacket that is patterned, this could be a great look for you for your holiday wedding. Because it is a classic piece, it is not as loud as, say, a multi-colored paisley printed blazer. We always advocate keeping it simple. Here, we chose a white tuxedo shirt, black grosgrain necktie, and matching black tuxedo pants and shoes to style with this blazer. We also added a gold collar pin to complement the buttons on the blazer. For a more detailed and dapper look, remember to coordinate hardware finishes when you are adding metal accessories to your look.

This Black Watch jacket is vintage. Vintage shopping is a great way to not only find one-of-a-kind pieces but also to save a bit of money. Some of the more boutique and specialized vintage stores have great selections, like this jacket. If you are not successful with a local vintage boutique, there are several ways to shop for vintage items online.

Master the Details

Tuxedo Shirt

To dress up the vintage blazer for your formal wedding, wear a tuxedo shirt with a pleated front instead of a standard white dress shirt, even though you will have on a necktie. Sometimes it is okay to make up your own rules and go against tradition.

Necktie

Choose a necktie for this look to add a modern element to an otherwise vintage look. Black grosgrain provides texture to the look, which is appropriate and sophisticated for a formal wedding.

Collar Pin

To keep the tuxedo shirt collar in place and add detailing, use a gold collar pin. Gold will work well because it matches the buttons on the vintage jacket. You always want to be consistent with those seemingly small details.

Tartans and Plaids

If you don't prefer Black Watch, or if it just does not work for your wedding, consider a blazer made from one of the other tartans or plaids that are popular during the holiday season.

Groomsmen

With this look, we recommend that your groomsmen wear black wool, notch lapel, suits accented with either solid black grosgrain or wool Black Watch neckties.

WHERE TO WEAR

The vintage Black Watch tartan blazer look is appropriate for a formal wedding with a vintage flair during the holiday season. We recommend the following venue types:

- Formal indoor wedding: country club, university club, library, or resort lodge

WAYS TO SAVE

- Purchasing a vintage blazer will likely result in some savings from the standard tuxedo jacket.

- Consider purchasing your black grosgrain necktie from an online retailer that may be less popular than some of the famous menswear designers. You can expect to save at least half the cost.

GET THE LOOK

Black Double-Breasted Waistcoat

White Dress Shirt with French Cuffs

Black Silk Self-Tie Bow Tie

Black Watch Tartan Slacks

Black Silk Knot Cufflinks

Black Silk Knot Stud Set

Silver Pocket Watch

Black Velvet Loafers

LOOK FOUR

Want to mix up your style a bit by making your pants the feature of your look? This is the first time in the book that we have explored formal pants with a pattern, but if we do say so ourselves, we like it! In this look, we put a black boiled wool, double-breasted waistcoat with Black Watch dress slacks. This is definitely for the fashion-forward groom who will stand confidently in his plaid pants. It is a departure from the norm but is certainly wedding appropriate.

Once again, since Black Watch plaid is a classic tartan, slacks in this material should be styled as if they are black tuxedo pants. This is why we styled them with a crisp white dress shirt with French cuffs, black bow tie, and a pocket watch. As an added touch, you could change the color of the silk knot buttons and cufflinks. We kept it simple and classic with black silk knot buttons and cufflinks, but dark green works, too. To really sharpen this look, we added a black velvet loafer, which was a great way to add texture to an overall sophisticated look. If you prefer to wear a classic black tuxedo for your wedding, this look could work equally well for your reception.

WHERE TO WEAR

This plaid pant look is a unique look for the Holiday Groom. We recommend the following venue types:

- Formal indoor wedding: hotel grand ballroom, country club, university club, grand library, or museum

- Formal outdoor wedding: historic home or city rooftop

WAYS TO SAVE

- Look for good quality dress shirts for you and your groomsmen at a local discount retailer. You may be able to find brand name shirts at a fraction of the cost. Before purchasing, confirm that the fabric, collar, and cuff style are appropriate for your wedding day look.

- Purchase your tartan dress slacks from a vintage boutique, and take them to your local tailor for the perfect fit.

Master the Details

Buttons
Typically, double-breasted waistcoats have columns of workable buttons and non-workable buttons. Etiquette says to always keep the last button of workable buttons unfastened.

Belt
Omit a belt with this look. Adding a belt in addition to the double-breasted waistcoat will be too much. Instead, have your pants tailored to your waist, so that a belt is not required.

Pocket Watch
A pocket watch is a fine detail to enhance this look. You can use a vintage heirloom or find a contemporary version. If you opt for the pocket watch, forego the wrist watch. Besides using it to keep time on your wedding day, it gives more of a dandy look than the standard wristwatch.

Fit
Fit is important with any slacks and even more with patterned, plaid, or tartan pants. If you can pull it off with your physique, we prefer a slim fit pant with little to no break at the shoe for the tartan pant. Pooling patterned fabric at the ankles will look very sloppy. Remember, on your wedding day, you want to be as dapper as possible.

Shoes
With a slim fit pant with no break, we prefer a loafer and no socks. If the velvet loafer, as shown here, is not your style, consider a calf-skin or patent leather loafer. Omitting socks keeps the look clean and focused on your stylish pants, instead of on your sock choice.

Groomsmen
Style your groomsmen in your same waistcoat, dress shirt, and bow tie combination. Switch the tartan pants for black dress slacks or tuxedo pants. You will be the only person in the tartan pants, which will clearly identify you as the groom.

THE
LOOK
FOR LESS

GET THE LOOK under $300

White French Cuff Dress Shirt,
Lauren by Ralph Lauren, **$69.50**

Velvet Five-Button Waistcoat,
*Kenneth Cole (purchased at
discount retailer),* **$19.99**

Houndstooth Self-Tie Bow Tie,
Polo Ralph Lauren, **$85.00**

Slim Fit Tuxedo Pants,
*Tommy Hilfiger (purchased at
discount retailer),* **$89.99**

Vintage Cufflinks,
NYC Flea Market, **$12.50**

Antique Gold Pocket Watch,
NYC Flea Market, **$15.00**

TOTAL **$291.98**

THE LOOK FOR LESS

We understand that weddings vary in budget—usually giving the groom's apparel a smaller allocation. It is most common that the groom spends significantly less than his bride for wedding day apparel, but no one needs to know that.

In addition to the "Ways to Save" items that have been highlighted in each section of the book, we wanted to delve further into the concept of looking good on any budget. The Mr. Baldwin Style brand is truly about the look for less, whenever possible. In this chapter, we want to bring special attention to some of the featured looks that were very sharp but did not cost a fortune. Getting the look for less is by no means about sacrificing quality because of a small budget. You won't always be able to find every low cost item for your wedding day, so you will need to mix high-priced items with low ones. High-priced items are usually by famous designers, whereas, low-priced items are usually by less notable designers.

In general, we feel that the splurge item for your wedding day should be your shoes. Not only will a quality pair of dress shoes elevate your look, but they should last for years. We have excluded shoes from the cost summaries in this chapter, as there are countless options for each look at different price levels. (A hint to you gentleman, women do pay attention to what's on your feet, so make sure you give them something good to see.)

GET THE LOOK under $300
The velvet waistcoat look is featured in "The Classic Groom" chapter. We recommended this look as a reception or second look for the groom at a classic style wedding. It can even work for the groomsmen when the groom is wearing a full tuxedo. This look is quite inexpensive because it is a mix of full-price designer items, sale items from discount retailers, and vintage finds.

Admittedly, it will take more time to go to various places to find all of the items than going to a tuxedo rental shop, but we think the result is worth it. You will still complement your bride's traditional gown while showing some of your personality in the process. There is very little predictability when it comes to vintage shopping. You really don't know what is going to be available; you just have to be willing to do the work and not be afraid to bargain with a vendor for an item that you really like.

GET THE LOOK under $400

Peak Lapel Tuxedo,
Discount Retailer, **$110.00**

Pink Custom-Fit Oxford Shirt
with Contrast Collar,
Polo Ralph Lauren, **$185.00**

Black Silk Self-Tie Bow Tie
Polo Ralph Lauren, **$85.00**

White Cotton Pocket Square,
Nordstrom Rack, **$4.00**

Floral Boutonnière,
Wedding Floral Designer, **$15.00**

TOTAL **$399**

The notch lapel tuxedo worn with the pink contrast collar dress shirt is one of the looks featured in "The Classic Groom Remixed" chapter. This look is an example of mixing high-priced and lower priced items. The higher ticket items are the designer dress shirt and bow tie; the lower priced items are the discount brand tuxedo and pocket square. With this look, we decided to style a notch lapel tuxedo by a discount brand with a dress shirt by a famous designer. The focal point of the look is the pink dress shirt and the black bow tie, so both need to be of good quality, fabric, and fit. The black tuxedo is of good quality, as well, but since the shirt was intended to stand out, it only needed to provide a backdrop for the pastel shirt. With an off-the-rack tuxedo, name brand or other, don't be shy about paying a visit to your tailor to achieve the perfect fit.

GET THE LOOK under $700

Blue and White Pincord Suit,
*Eaden Myles "Hampton Boy"
Custom Suit*, **$589.99**

Slim Fit Pink Oxford Shirt,
Polo Ralph Lauren, **$89.00**

Navy Diamond Tip Bow Tie,
Save on Ties, **$14.99**

White Pocket Square,
Nordstrom Rack, **$4.00**

TOTAL **$697.98**

The blue and white pincord suit look was featured in "The Preppy Groom" chapter. This ensemble, as shown, can be purchased for just under $700. The pincord suit is a nice departure from the classic black tuxedo when appropriate. The suit is made-to-measure which is a great option for achieving a tailored look without the cost of a bespoke suit. The pink shirt is off-the-rack but can be tailored, if required. In a warmer climate, there are certain times during the reception when you may want to remove your suit jacket, and the last thing you want to do is to show a baggy, loose-fitting dress shirt. While the suit and dress shirt costs are low to mid-range, the bow tie and pocket square are very low in cost, coming in at less than $20. When styled with the pincord suit and dress shirt, no one will ever know that these items are inexpensive.

GET THE LOOK under $850

Gray Peak Lapel Suit,
Eaden Myles "Euro II" Custom Suit,
$589.99

Custom-Tailored Tuxedo Shirt,
Eaden Myles, **$159.99**

Gray Knit Tie, *Save on Ties*, **$13.99**

Bloom Lapel Pin in Gray,
Fleur'd Pins, **$38.00**

Black Socks (optional item), **$7.99**

TOTAL $809.96

The gray peak lapel suit is one of our features from the "Chic Groom" chapter and is very versatile yet appropriate for many contemporary wedding settings. This entire look can be achieved for under $850. We have featured this look in the "Look for Less" chapter because it is a custom-fit look that can be achieved without spending a fortune.

The made-to-measure suit and tuxedo shirt are great options for achieving the perfect fit, as they are tailored to fit your measurements. Likewise, your bride's gown will likely be made to measure, as well. Together, you will both have clothing that complements your physiques, which will allow your guests to see the effort you put into achieving your polished look.

The gray knit tie and bloom lapel pin are added accents that keep the monochromatic theme and are slightly over $50. It is hard to go wrong with this sharp, tailored look that will cost less than $850.

STYLING TIPS & PLANNING

INTERVIEW ON MEN'S GROOMING

Another component to ensure a dapper look on your wedding day is grooming. In addition to your perfectly selected outfit with the impeccable fit, we want to make sure that your skin, hair, and nails all look their best on your wedding day. We interviewed renowned men's grooming expert, Scott McMahan, to get his tips for the modern groom. Scott, based in New York City, is one of the most sought after groomers in men's fashion, daily working with well-known models and photographers. See below for his tips on how to get prepared for your big day.

MR. BALDWIN STYLE: What is a good skincare routine a groom should implement leading up to his wedding?

SCOTT MCMAHAN: Every guy, not just the marrying kind, should spend a little time finding the right combination of skincare products and techniques that work best for him and his skin type. While it might not sound fun or very interesting, the payoff can be noticeably great. Even if he opts to keep it as simple as possible, everyone should make it a habit to cleanse and moisturize every day, and exfoliate once or twice a week.

MBS: When should a groom get his haircut in preparation for his wedding day?

SM: I always recommend getting a fresh cut about five or six days before the wedding. It will give the cut a chance to settle a bit and will allow time to even out any tan lines that might be left exposed after the haircut. Also, accidents can happen.

You will have time to decide how best to deal with a not-so-kind cut. Of course, if the groom is used to getting very regular cuts and keeping a tight look, by all means, get a cut a couple of days before, or even the morning of the wedding.

MBS: When should a groom shave prior to his wedding day?

SM: When to shave really depends on the look he wants for the wedding. He should think about how smooth or scruffy he wants to look and how fast his beard grows, and then shave at the appropriate time. Think about going with the look you most often wear. If you always have a beard, I wouldn't suggest suddenly shaving the day of the wedding. But if the beard has to go, try shaving regularly for a few weeks prior to the wedding. You will be less likely to experience an angry skin reaction after shaving on the big day.

MBS: How do you recommend getting the perfect shave?

SM: I think the most important thing a guy can do to help get a more perfect shave is *take his time*. Start with freshly cleansed skin, and then lather up, and leave it for a few minutes. The wait will optimize the softening action from the shaving foam, gel, or cream. I like using a double blade razor going *with the grain*, the direction your hair grows. Sure, you can get a closer shave by going against nature, but the risk of ingrown hairs is high. Nobody wants ingrown hairs on their face, especially on their wedding day.

MBS: What grooming product is worth a splurge?

SM: A great fragrance! That drugstore body spray won't really cut it on your wedding day, or any other day for that matter. Do some sampling of different kinds of scents to find the type you like best, and then shop around to find exactly the right one for you. Remember, a little goes a long way.

MBS: Should a groom get a manicure and pedicure before the wedding?

SM: Whether he decides to go to a professional to get his nail care on or not, every groom should spend some quality time on his hands and feet. After all, he is about to do a lot of handshaking. Plus, I guarantee that there's one important person who will appreciate that he got those claws clipped before the wedding night.

MBS: Should a groom 'manscape' before the wedding?

SM: To manscape or not to manscape? That's really a personal preference in this situation. But, they do say, "There's nothing like trimming the bush to make the tree look bigger." Again, it's your *wedding night!*

We are thankful for Scott's advice and his humor, too. On your wedding day, you want to present the best version of yourself. Take a little time leading up to the wedding to plan how you will prepare your skin, nails, and hair for the big day. You won't regret it, and your bride will be even happier with the groomed gentleman waiting at the other end of the aisle for her.

HOW TO WEAR A TUXEDO (visual guide)

1. Your dress shirt or tuxedo shirt collar should fit at the neck with only enough room to get your index and middle fingers in the collar of the shirt.

2. Get a self-tie bow tie, and learn to tie it.

3. Choose a pocket square and the appropriate fold. (Here, a white pocket square with a presidential or square fold is shown.)

4. The tuxedo jacket should fit well at the shoulders. If your shoulder muscles bulge out past the shoulder pads of the jacket, it is too small.

5. The jacket should fit the body and arms without being too small.

6. When your arms are at your sides, ¼" to ½" of your shirtsleeves should show beyond the sleeve of the tuxedo jacket.

7. Tuxedo pants should fit the entire leg without it being too loose or too tight, hugging your thighs or calves.

8. Have your tuxedo pants hemmed with an appropriate break at your shoes or boots. Tuxedo pants should never have a cuff. (Here, the pants have a minimal break.)

HOW TO WEAR A SUIT (visual guide)

1. Your dress shirt collar should fit at the neck with only enough room to get your index and middle fingers in the collar of the shirt.

2. The suit jacket should fit well at the shoulders. If your shoulder muscles bulge out past the shoulder pads of the jacket, it is too small.

3. If wearing a necktie, make sure to fasten the top button of the shirt.

4. Tie your necktie snug enough to cover the top button of the dress shirt, and leave it long enough to meet the top of the waistband on your pants.

5. Place a dimple in your necktie right below the tie knot.

6. Place the collar pin beneath the necktie, and connect the two ends of the shirt collar. With a button-down collar shirt, we prefer to leave the buttons unfastened.

7. Place the tie clip between the third and fourth buttons from the top of the dress shirt.

8. Place the boutonnière on the left lapel of the jacket covering the lapel buttonhole.

9. Choose a pocket square and the appropriate fold. (Here, a printed silk pocket square is shown with a three-point fold.)

10. Button only the top button when wearing a two-button suit.

11. When your arms are at your sides, ¼" to ½" of your shirtsleeves should show beyond the sleeve of the suit jacket.

12. Suit pants should fit the entire leg without being too loose or too tight, hugging your thighs or calves.

13. Have your suit pants hemmed with an appropriate break at your shoes or boots. (Here, the pants are shown with no break.)

LEVELS OF FORMALITY FOR WEDDING DAY ATTIRE

As mentioned in the "Getting Started" section of the book, there are varying levels of formality for wedding day attire. The following are some examples of menswear items for a groom and/or his attendants that correspond with each level. Attire for the guests may vary slightly.

CASUAL
Acceptable: collared shirts, chino slacks, denim, and leather shoes

Optional: casual blazer, sport coat, waistcoat, and boots

Not Required: tuxedo, suit, necktie, and bow tie

SEMI FORMAL
Acceptable: tailored suit, necktie, and leather dress shoes

Optional: double-breasted suit jacket, braces, bow tie, and dress boots

Not Required: tuxedo jacket, tuxedo pants, and cummerbund

FORMAL
Acceptable: darker colored, tailored suit (black, navy, or gray), necktie, navy or other colored tuxedo, and leather or patent leather dress shoes

Optional: double-breasted suit jacket, tuxedo shirt, braces, bow tie, and dress boots

Not Required: black tuxedo and white dinner jacket

BLACK TIE
Acceptable: black tuxedo, white dinner jacket, tuxedo shirt, stud set, and patent leather tie-up shoes or loafers

Optional: waistcoat, cummerbund, colored pocket square, leather shoes, and velvet loafers

Not Required: tailcoat

WHITE TIE
Acceptable: white waistcoat, black evening coat with tails, black slacks, and white bow tie

Optional: wing-collar tuxedo shirt,

Not Required: black bow tie

WEDDING DAY APPAREL TIMELINE

Three to Four Months Prior to the Wedding

Review the items listed in the "Getting Started" section of the book to begin brainstorming about your wedding day attire.

If you are stumped on what to wear or you and your bride cannot settle on a look, consult a groom's wardrobe stylist, like Mr. Baldwin Style. This type of stylist can prepare guided looks and a mood board with inspiration for your attire that will help you as you search.

Begin thinking about your groomsmen's wedding day attire. When selecting the items for your groomsmen to purchase, be considerate of how much they will need to spend. Remember this is your wedding, not theirs. It is fine to consult with them about the budget before you make apparel selections.

Two to Three Months Prior to the Wedding

Begin shopping for your wedding day apparel (in particular, your suit or tuxedo) either on your own or with your wardrobe stylist. We recommend starting the process during this time period just in case your desired tuxedo or suit must be ordered.

If you select a tuxedo or suit to be custom made, typically the lead time (fabrication and delivery) is about six weeks. Therefore, make sure you complete your measurement appointments and place the order in enough time to leave leeway for any unforeseen delays. If your groomsmen will be wearing custom items, their orders should be placed, as well.

One Month Prior to the Wedding

If you have not settled on a tuxedo or suit yet, consider selecting an off-the-rack item that can be tailored for the proper fit.

Once you have identified your tuxedo or suit, settle on the same for your groomsmen. If all of you are wearing the same tuxedo or suit, make sure that the retailer has adequate inventory and sizing to accommodate your wedding party. If not, you may have to choose something else.

Shop for any remaining accoutrements (pocket square, tie, lapel, etc.), including your shoes.

Two to Three Weeks Prior to the Wedding

If you have purchased an off-the-rack tuxedo or suit, take it to a local tailor for alterations. Make sure that you give clear details regarding your desired fit.

If your groomsmen have also purchased items off-the-rack and are taking it to a different tailor from yours, make sure you give your groomsmen clear direction on the desired fit. For example, make sure you indicate cuff or no cuff for the suit pants

One to Two Weeks Prior to the Wedding

If you have ordered a custom tuxedo or suit, pick it up from the custom suit retailer. Make sure to try it on just in case you need any small alterations. Your groomsmen should complete this step, as well.

If you purchased off-the-rack and dropped off your tuxedo or suit with a local tailor, pick up your items. Try on the tuxedo or suit to make sure you are happy with the fit.

The Day Before the Wedding

Steam your entire look, including your tie and pocket square.

Wedding Day

If you will be traveling a distance to your wedding venue, make sure to bring your apparel to the venue in a garment bag and change in the designated location on site to avoid any wrinkles or stains.

Relax! The hard part is done. Enjoy this day and all that will come with marrying your bride!

AVOID COMMON MISTAKES ON YOUR WEDDING DAY

- Your boutonnière or lapel pin should always be placed on the left lapel of your suit or tuxedo jacket. Make sure that the boutonnière or lapel pin is placed on the lapel of the jacket (on its buttonhole) not on the face of the jacket above the pocket.

- If you are wearing a floral boutonnière, then skip the lapel pin, and vice versa. You only need one.

- If you are wearing a necktie, make sure to button the top button of your shirt and adjust the necktie to cover the top button. Also, make sure to create a dimple in the tie just below the knot. A dimple is the sign of a savvy gentleman.

- If you are wearing a necktie, make sure the tip of the tie falls right below the waistband of the pants, covering the button or fastener. Avoid making the tie too long or too short.

- If you are wearing a bow tie (we prefer the self-tie versions), make sure that the bow tie covers the top button of the dress shirt and is on straight.

- If you are wearing a pocket square, make sure the fold is appropriately sized within your pocket. The pocket square should not be falling out or too low.

- Select a belt or braces (suspenders). Wearing both is redundant and will look odd. Note that properly tailored suit pants do not require a belt (even if the pants have belt loops).

- Make sure to neatly tuck your shirt into your pants. Try to avoid too much of the shirt blousing out of your pants.

- Make sure the zipper on your slacks is up.

- If you are wearing socks, make sure they are ones that you are okay with people seeing. Your wedding day is not the time to try to hide a gym sock or neon sock underneath your slacks.

- Try to stick with a more formal shoe for the ceremony. If you must wear sneakers, consider making them a reception look that you switch into after the ceremony. To perfect this look, make sure your pant length has been altered to accommodate both pairs of shoes appropriately.

- If you are wearing a tuxedo or suit jacket, anytime you are standing up, your jacket should be buttoned. This includes standing at the altar, taking wedding photos, cutting your wedding cake, or formally greeting your guests. Remember the button rules, if you are wearing a two button suit, you *always* button

the top button and *never* the bottom button. If you are wearing a three-button suit, we prefer to button the middle button only. The top button is optional and never the bottom one. If wearing a waistcoat, the last button should always remain unbuttoned.

- If you are wearing a tuxedo or suit jacket, anytime that you are seated, your jacket should be unbuttoned. This includes during dinner or wedding toasts.

- Do not wear sunglasses during your wedding ceremony. Your bride, the officiant, and your guests want to see your eyes. Save the sunglasses for your honeymoon.

- If you have selected a fashion hat as an accessory to your wedding day look, make sure that you don't wear the hat during the wedding ceremony. Consider using the hat as an accessory during your wedding photos or after-party.

HEAD-TO-TOE CHECK BEFORE THE CEREMONY

To make sure you are at your best on your special day, complete this quick head-to-toe check right before the ceremony:

HAIR Check that your hair has been brushed or combed to your liking.

EYES Check that that there is no crust or mucus.

NOSE Check that there are no unwanted "friends" coming from your nose.

FACIAL HAIR Check that your facial hair is clean-shaven and well-groomed.

TEETH Check that there is no food or particles in your teeth.

TIE Check the dimple near the knot, if you are wearing a necktie. Make sure the top button is fastened and covered by the tie. If you are wearing a bow tie, make sure it is properly aligned.

JACKET Check that the appropriate buttons are fastened.

LAPEL Check that it is flat and not flipped.

LAPEL PIN / FLORAL BOUTONNIÈRE Check that it has been placed in the correct location.

POCKET SQUARE / HANDKERCHIEF Check that it is not sitting too high or low.

SHIRT BUTTONS Check that all of the appropriate buttons are fastened, including the sleeves.

BELT / SUSPENDERS Check that you have one or the other, not both. With braces, check that they are not too loose or tight.

ZIPPER Check to make sure it is zipped.

UNDERWEAR Check that they are not visible through your clothing. This includes undershirts. If your skin tone is darker, use a gray or black undershirt.

PANTS / SLACKS Check the placement on your waist, and make sure they fall appropriately without static.

SOCKS Check that the socks have been pulled up so that no skin is visible at the bottom of your pants.

SHOES Check that your shoes have been shined and are laced.